THE BIGGEST BOOK OF STUPID JOKES IN THE UNIVERSE

David Mostyn

Robinson Children's Books

Robinson Publishing Ltd
7 Kensington Church Court
London W8 4SP

First published in the UK by Robinson Children's Books,
an imprint of Robinson Publishing Ltd, 1998

A copy of the British Library Cataloguing in Publication
Data for this title is available from the British Library.

ISBN 1 85487 632 5

Printed and bound in the EC

10 9 8 7 6 5 4 3 2 1

INTRODUCTION

Congratulations on buying *The Biggest Book of Stupid Jokes in the Universe*! This collection includes every type of joke created by mankind – from the wackiest one-liners, classroom capers, riddles and Knock knock jokes to stories that keep you guessing – and groaning! Here's a selection to get you in the mood.

Why did the golfer wear an extra pair of trousers?
In case he got a hole in one.

Why did Ken keep his trumpet in the fridge?
Because he liked cool music.

Why is history like a fruit cake?
Because it's full of dates.

What did the mother ghost say to the naughty baby ghost?
Spook when you're spooken to.

"Dad, when I get old will the calves of my legs be cows?"

The wonderful Wizard of Oz
Retired from business becoz
What with up to date science
To most of his clients
He wasn't the wiz that he woz.

And for those who like bananas…

"They're not going to grow bananas any longer."
"Really? Why not?"
"Because they're long enough already."

Why didn't the banana snore?
'Cos it was afraid to wake up the rest of the bunch.

Did you hear about the posh school where all the pupils smelt?
It was for filthy rich kids only.

"How would you measure the height of the Eiffel Tower with an aneroid barometer, Jim?"
"I'd tie a long piece of string to it, and throw it off the top. When it hit the ground, I'd measure the string."

"Please Sir!" said a new boy at school to his teacher.
"Why is your name the same as the headmaster's?"
"Because he's my father!"
"Did you know that when you took the job, Sir?"

Why is the school swot like quick sand?
Because everything in school sinks into him.

I used to be thin.
Now I'm thinner.
So would you be
With our school dinner.

What are pupils at ghost schools called?
Ghoulboys and ghoulgirls.

Two schoolboys were talking about their arithmetic
lessons.
"Why do you suppose we stop the tables at 12?"
asked one.
"Oh, don't you know," said the other. "I heard Mum say
it was unlucky to have 13 at table."

Jim turned up for football practice clutching a large
broom.
"What's that for?" asked the coach.
"You said I was going to be sweeper today."

"Ann! Point out Australia for me on the map."
Ann went to the front of the class, picked up the
pointer and showed the rest of the class where
Australia was.
"Well done! Now, Jim! Can you tell us who discovered
Australia?"
"Er . . . Ann, Miss?"

"Teacher is a bore!" was scrawled on the blackboard
one day.
"I do not want to see that on my blackboard," he
thundered when he saw it. "Sorry, Sir! I didn't realize
you wanted it kept secret."

Found in the school library:
The Broken Window by Eva Brick
Gone Shopping by Carrie R. Bag
The Short Break by T.N. Biscuits
Me and the Wife by Ian Shee
Mexican Cookery by Gilly con Carne
The Lady Ghost by Sheila Peer
The Rich Man's Guide to Good Living by Ivor Lot
Cooking with Pork by Chris P. Bacon
Cry Baby by Liza Weeping

"Lie flat on your backs, class, and circle your feet in the air as if you were riding your bikes" said the gym teacher. "Jim! What are you doing? Move your feet, boy."
"I'm freewheeling, Sir."

"What were you before you came to school, boys and girls?" asked the teacher, hoping that someone would say "babies."
She was disappointed when all the children cried out, "Happy!"

Did you hear about the schoolboy who just couldn't get to grips with decimals?
He couldn't see the point.

"Jean, define a baby."
"A soft pink thing that makes a lot of noise at one end and has no sense of responsibility at the other."

"In some countries," said the geography teacher, "men are allowed more than one wife. That's called polygamy. In others, women are allowed more than one husband. That's called polyandry. In this country, men and women are allowed only one married partner. Can anyone tell me what that's called?"

"Monotony, Sir!"

"Why are you tearing up your homework notebook and scattering the pieces around the playground?" a furious teacher asked one of her pupils.

"To keep the elephants away, Miss."

"There are no elephants."

"Shows how effective it is then, doesn't it?"

"Don't worry Miss Jones," said the headmaster to the new teacher. "You'll cope with your new class, but they'll keep you on your toes."

"How's that, Sir?" asked the teacher.

"They always put thumbtacks on the chairs."

What's the difference between teachers and candy?
People like candy.

"Why are you crying, Jim?" asked the teacher.

"Cos my parrot died last night. I washed it in Persil."

"Jim," said the teacher. "You must have known that Persil's bad for parrots."

"Oh it wasn't the Persil that killed it, Sir. It was the spin drier."

Knock, knock.
Who's there?
Teacher.
Teacher who?
Teacher-self French.

What's the difference between a railway guard and a teacher?
One minds the train, the other trains the mind.

"I see you've got that new boy down for the football game against Brick Street," said the English teacher to the games master.
"Yes, but I'm not sure what position to play him."
"Well, if his football's anything like his English he's a natural drawback."

"Can anyone think of a vegetable that's mentioned in the Bible?" asked the English teacher.
"Lettuce, Sir," said Jim.
"I don't think so, Jim," the teacher said.
"Oh yes, Sir," protested Jim. "Someone says, 'Lettuce with a gladsome mind praise the Lord for he is kind.' "

"What are the elements, Jim?" asked the science teacher.
"Er . . . earth . . . air . . . fire . . ."
"Well done," said the teacher. "There's one more."
"Er . . . oh yes. Golf."
"Golf!"
"Yes, I heard my mum say that dad's in his element when he plays golf."

When Bud, an American boy, visited an English school the games teacher asked Jim to explain the rules of cricket to him. "Well," said Jim, "there are two sides, one out in the field and one in the pavilion. Each man in the side that's in goes out and when he's out he comes in and the next man goes in until he's out. When they're all out, the side that's been out comes in and the side that's been in goes out and tries to get the players coming in, out. When both sides have been in and out, including the not-outs, that's the end of the game." "Thanks" said Bud. "I'll stick to baseball."

"Some educationalists think that in all-boy junior schools the boys are more intelligent than girls in all-girl junior schools, but in all-boy senior schools, the pupils are less intelligent than girls in all-girl senior schools."
"What's that? What about co-educational senior schools?"
"Oh the boys and girls are neck and neck there."

"Jim," groaned his father when he saw his son's school report. "Why are you so awful at geography?" "It's the teacher's fault, Dad. He keeps telling us about places I've never heard of."

Jim gave his father his school report one night. Dad was pleased to read that Jim's handwriting had improved tremendously. "But sadly," wrote the English teacher, "the improvement in the legibility of Jim's handwriting has revealed a great deficiency in his spelling ability."

I'm not saying our teacher's fat, but every time he falls over he rocks himself to sleep trying to get back up.

"Jim," said the religious education teacher, "you've written here that Samson was an actor. What makes you think that?"
"Well Sir," said Jim, "I read that he brought the house down."

"You can have that brain there for $3,000," said the brain surgeon to the man who was going to have a brain transplant. "It used to belong to a bank manager. This one's $5,000: it was a dancer's. And this one's $50,000: it belonged to a school teacher."
"Why's it ten times more than the others?" gasped the man.
"It's been used ten times less than theirs!"

Why did the singing teacher have such a high-pitched voice?
She had falsetto teeth.

"And what might your name be?" the school secretary asked the new boy.
"Well it might be Cornelius, but it's not. It's Sam."

13

What happens if there's a collision outside school?
There's usually a fight.

What happened to the baby chicken that misbehaved at school?
It was eggspelled.

Teacher: I was going to read you a story called *The Invasion of the Body Snatchers*, but I've changed my mind.
Class: Oh why, Miss?
Teacher: Because we might get carried away.

"Ann," said the dancing mistress. "There are two things stopping you becoming the world's greatest ballerina."
"What are they, Miss?" asked Ann.
"Your feet."

"I hope you're not one of those boys who sits and watches the school clock," said the principal to a new boy.
"No, Sir. I've got a digital watch that bleeps at half past three."

"Who was that I saw you with last night?"
"It was a girl from the school."
"Teacher?"
"Didn't have to!"

Generally speaking, teachers are generally speaking.

At a very posh boarding school, one of the teachers who was going out for a grand dinner appeared wearing a dinner jacket, evening shirt and black tie. "Oh Sir," said one of the boys. "You're not wearing those clothes are you? You know they always give you a headache in the morning."

"Mary," said her teacher. "You can't bring that lamb into school. What about the smell?"
"Oh, that's all right, Miss," said Mary. "It'll soon get used to it."

What's the definition of a school report?
A poison pen letter from the principal.

Why did the football teacher give his team lighters?
Because they kept losing all their matches.

"I told you to draw a picture of a cow eating grass,"
said the art master. "Why have you handed in a blank
sheet of paper?"
"Because the cow ate all the grass, that's why there's
no grass."
"But what about the cow?"
"There wasn't much point in it hanging around when
there was nothing to eat, so he went back to the byre."

A little boy ran home from school on the first day and
pestered his mother into taking him into a toy shop.
When they got there he insisted that she buy him a
gun.
"But why do you need a gun?" asked his mother.
"Because teacher told us she was going to teach us to
draw tomorrow."

"That's an excellent essay for someone your age," said
the English teacher.
"How about for someone my Mom's age, Miss?"

Why wouldn't the skeleton go to school?
Because his heart wasn't in it.

"Mommy," said the little lamb. "Can I go to an all-ram's school when I'm five?"

"Don't be silly, darling," said his mother who was a very aristocratic sheep. "That would be frightfully non-U."

A chemist, a shopkeeper and a teacher were sentenced to death by firing squad. The chemist was taken from his cell and as the soldiers took aim he shouted "Avalanche!" The soldiers panicked and in the confusion the chemist escaped.

The shopkeeper was led out next. As the soldiers took aim he shouted "Flood!" and escaped.

The teacher was then led out. The squad took aim and the teacher, remembering how the other two had escaped, shouted "Fire!"

Teachers nowadays specialize so much that they know more and more about less and less until they know everything about nothing!

"It was *Hamlet*," a boarding-school boy wrote to his parents after the school play. "Most of the other boys' parents had seen it before, but they laughed just the same."

Did you hear about the teacher whose pupils were all swots? When she walked into the classroom and said "Good morning" they wrote it in their notebooks.

There once was a schoolboy named Rhett,
Who ate ten Mars Bars for a bet.
When asked "Are you faint?"
He said, "No I ain't.
But I don't feel like flying a jet."

There was once a lad called Willy Maufe.
When he went to school for the first time the teacher
asked him his name.
"I'm Maufe," said Willy.
"Don't be silly, boy," said the teacher. "You'll stay here
till 3.30 like the rest of us."

"Well, children," said the cannibal cookery teacher.
"What did you make of the new English teacher?"
"Burgers, Miss."

"Where's your pencil, Bud?" the teacher asked an
American boy who had just come to school.
"I ain't got one, Sir."
"You're in England now, Bud. Not "ain't," "haven't."
I haven't got a pencil. You haven't got a pencil. They
haven't got a pencil."
"Gee!" said Bud. "Pop said things were tough in this
country, but I didn't know pencils were so hard to come
by."

Mr Anderson, the science teacher, was very absent-minded. One day he brought a box into the classroom and said, "I've got a frog and a toad in here. When I get them out we'll look at the differences."
He put his hand into the box and pulled out two sandwiches.
"Oh dear!" he said. "I could have sworn I'd just had my lunch."

One day a teacher came into her classroom and found a very rude word chalked on her blackboard.
"I'm not going to scold," she said. "We're going to take care of this by the honor system. We'll all close our eyes and I'll count up to 100. When we open our eyes whoever wrote that will have tiptoed up to the board and erased it."
Everyone closed their eyes. "One . . . two . . . three . . . pitter patter . . . 48 . . . 49 . . . 50 . . . squeak, squeak . . . 99, 100."
Everyone opened their eyes and there, on the board, was another, even filthier word and above it was chalked, "The phantom writer strikes again."

"Did you thank Mrs Pillbeam for teaching you today?" Alec's mum asked him when he came home from school.
"No I didn't. Mary in front of me did and Mrs Pillbeam said, 'Don't mention it,' so I didn't."

What's the difference between school dinners and a bucket of fresh manure?
School dinners are usually cold.

Why wouldn't the skeleton go to the ghoul's school disco?
He had no body to go with.

Did you hear about the cross-eyed teacher who had no control over her pupils?

What's the longest piece of furniture in the school?
The multiplication table.

Did you hear what happened when there was an epidemic of laryngitis at school?
The school nurse sent everyone to the croakroom.

When Dad came home he was astonished to see Jim sitting on a horse, writing something.
"What on earth are you doing there?" he asked.
"Well, teacher told us to write an essay on our favorite animal. That's why I'm here and that's why Susie's sitting in the goldfish bowl."

How do Religious Education teachers mark exams?
With spirit levels.

The games teacher, Miss Janet Rockey
Wanted to train as a jockey.
But, sad to recall,
She grew far too tall.
So now she teaches us hockey.

Janet came home from school and asked her mother if
the aerosol spray in the kitchen was hair lacquer.
"No," said Mom. "It's glue."
"I thought so," said Janet. "I wondered why I couldn't
get my hat off today."

Little Tommy was the quietest boy in school. He never
answered any questions but his homework was always
quite excellent. If anyone said anything to him he
would simply nod, or shake his head.
The staff thought he was shy and decided to do
something to give him confidence.
"Tommy," said his teacher. "I've just bet Miss Smith $5
I can get you to say three words. You can have half."
Tommy looked at her pityingly and said, "You lose."

A very new and very nervous school inspector was being shown round a very rough school. Just as the tour of inspection was coming to an end, the principal asked him if he'd mind saying a few words of advice to a class of unruly 16-year-olds who were going to leave school at the end of term.

The principal managed to get the kids to be quiet, introduced them to the inspector and told them that he was going to say a few words to them.

The poor man was totally nonplussed by the sight of the unwelcoming faces staring at him, but he took a deep breath and began:

"When y.y.y.ou were in.in.in.fants I'm sure you enjoyed your in.in.in.infancy. As ch.ch.ch.children I'm sure you enjoyed y.y.y.your ch.ch.childhood. I c.c.c.can see that you are enjoying your a.a.a.a.dolescence and I h.h.h.ope that wh.wh.when you l.l.l.l.leave school and become adults, you will enjoy your adultery."

Thinking he would play a trick on the biology teacher, Jim glued a beetle's head to a caterpillar's body and very carefully attached some butterfly wings and ant's legs.

The teacher was very impressed. "I've never seen anything like this, Jim," he said. "Tell me. Did it hum when you caught it?"

"Why yes, Sir. Quite loudly."

"I thought so. It's a humbug."

I enjoy doing my homework
Even at weekends,
But my best friend's just told me
He thinks I'm round the bend.

"Welcome to school, Simon," said the nursery school teacher to the new boy. "How old are you?"
"I'm not old," said Simon. "I'm nearly new."

"Please Miss!" said a little boy at kindergarten. "We're going to play elephants and circuses, do you want to join in?"
"I'd love to," said the teacher. "What do you want me to do?"
"You can be the lady that feeds us peanuts!"

What's the difference between an angler and a schoolboy?
One baits his hooks. The other hates his books.

What do you get if you cross old potatoes with lumpy mince?
School dinners.

A girl who was at a very expensive school turned up on her parents' doorstep one night, very distressed.
"Daddy," she sobbed. "I's just been expelled . . ."
"Hell's Bells!" exploded her father. "$5,000 a term and she still says 'I's.' "

Miss Jones who teaches us math,
Isn't much of a laugh.
For, sad to tell,
She doesn't half smell,
For she never has taken a bath.

Did you hear about the teacher who married the dairy maid?
It didn't last. They were like chalk and cheese.

"Why are you crying, Amanda?" asked her teacher.
" 'Cos Jenny's broken my new doll, Miss," she cried.
"How did she do that?"
"I hit her on the head with it."

The night-school teacher asked one of his pupils when he had last sat an exam.
"1945," said the lad.
"Good lord! That's more than 40 years ago."
"No Sir! An hour and half, it's quarter past nine now."

"I'd like you to be very quiet today, boys and girls. I've got a dreadful headache."
"Please Miss!" said Jim. "Why don't you do what Mom does when she has a headache?"
"What's that?"
"She sends us out to play."

"Mommy," sobbed the little girl. "I told teacher that great-great grandpapa died at Waterloo, and she said, 'Really, which platform?' and everybody giggled."
"Well next time she says that you just tell her that the platform number is irrelevant."

Did you hear about the teacher who retired?
His class gave him an illuminated address. They
burned his house down.

Confucius he say: If teacher ask you question and you
not know answer, mumble.

*What did the arithmetic book say to the geometry
book?*
Boy! Do we have our problems!

Games mistress: Come on, Sophie. You can run faster
than that.
Sophie: I can't, Miss. I'm wearing run-resistant tights.

Why was the little bird expelled from school?
She was always playing practical yolks.

An English teacher asked her class to write an essay on what they'd do if they had $1,000,000. Jim handed in a blank sheet of paper.

"Jim!" yelled the teacher. "You've done nothing. Why?"

" 'Cos if I had $1,000,000 that's exactly what I would do."

Why are American schoolchildren extremely healthy?
Because they have a good constitution.

A teacher was being interviewed for a new job and asked the principal what the hours were.

"We try to have early hours, you know. I hope that suits."

"Of course," said the teacher. "I don't mind how early I leave."

"And what's your name?" the secretary asked the next new boy.

"Butter."

"I hope your first name's not Roland," smirked the secretary.

"No, Miss. It's Brendan."

"What's your first name?" the teacher asked a new boy.

It's Orson, Miss. I was named after Orson Welles, the film star."

"Just as well your last name's not Cart. Isn't it?"

"Yes, Miss. It's Trapp."

A little girl was next in line. "My name's Curtain," she said.

"I hope your first name's not Annette?"

"No. It's Velvet."

Did you hear about the math teacher who fainted in class?

Everyone tried to bring her 2.

I smother school dinner with lots of honey.

I've done it all my life.

It makes the food taste funny.

But the peas stay on my knife.

Knock, knock.

Who's there?

Canoe.

Canoe who?

Canoe help me with my homework, please, Dad. I'm stuck.

What do you call an English teacher, five feet tall, covered from head to toe in boils and totally bald?

Sir!

"Teacher reminds me of the sea," said Jim to Billy.
"You mean she's deep, sometimes calm but occasionally stormy?"
"No! She makes me sick."

Why did the math teacher take a ruler to bed with him?
He wanted to see how long he would sleep.

Your daughter's only five and she can spell her name backwards? Why, that is remarkable." The headmistress was talking to a parent who was trying to impress her with the child's academic prowess so that she would be accepted into the school.
"Yes, we're very proud of her," said the mother.
"And what is your daughter's name?"
"Anna."

Principal: "If you liked your pupils you'd take them to the zoo."
Teacher: "Oh, I know some of them come from sub-standard houses, but they can't be that bad, surely."

"The girl beside me in math is very clever," said Jim to his mother. "She's got enough brains for two."
"Perhaps you'd better think about marriage," said Mom.

"Dad," said Billy to his father who was a bank robber. "I need $50 for the school trip tomorrow."

"OK, son," said his dad, "I'll get you the cash when the bank closes."

"I'm very sad to announce this morning, boys and girls, that Miss Jones has decided to retire," said the principal at morning assembly. "Now we will all stand and sing this morning's hymn . . . 'Now Thank We All Our God.'"

Did you hear about the Irish schoolboy who was studying Greek Mythology? When the teacher asked him to name something that was half-man and half-beast he replied,
"Buffalo Bill."

Svenda Norselander, a girl from Lapland, came to our school for a term.

"We have geography lessons first," said the teacher.

"I am not knowing the geography," said Svenda.

"How about history?"

"I am not knowing the history."

"Domestic science?"

"What is this domestic science?"

"Chemistry? Physics? Botany?"

"I know not what these things are."

"What do you know?" asked the teacher, trying to keep her temper.

"I am knowing how to breed the reindeer."

That was the last straw.

"We don't need to breed rain here!" cried the teacher. "We have enough already. And don't be so familiar with me on your first day."

Rich boy to dinner lady: "This bread's horrible. Why can't you make your own bread like the servants do at home?"
Dinner lady: "Because we don't have the kind of dough that your father makes!"

"Who was Captain Kidd?" asked the history teacher.
"He was a contortionist."
"What makes you think that, Jim?"
"Well it says in the history book that he spent a lot of time sitting on his chest."

When the school was broken into, the thieves took absolutely everything – desks, books, blackboards, everything apart from the soap in the lavatories and all the towels.
The police are looking for a pair of dirty criminals.

The principal was very proud of his school's academic record.
"It is very impressive," said one parent who was considering sending his son there. "How do you maintain such high standards?"
"Simple," said the head. "The school motto says it all."
"What's that?" asked the parent.
"If at first you don't succeed, you're expelled."

What's the difference between a boring teacher and a boring book?
You can shut the book up.

Teacher: "That's the stupidest boy in the whole school."
Mother: "That's my son."
Teacher: "Oh! I'm so sorry."
Mother: "*You're* sorry?"

Two parents were waiting at the school gate. "Look at that teacher," said one to the other. "It's disgraceful. Jeans. A rugby shirt. Trainers. Cropped blue hair. You'd never think she was a teacher, would you?"
"Well I would actually. That's my child. We're meeting here to go shopping together."
"Oh I'm sorry. I didn't realize you were her mother."
"I'm not. I'm her father actually! And she's my son!"

Typing teacher: "Bob! Your work has certainly improved. There are only ten mistakes here."
Bob: "Oh good, Miss."
Teacher: "Now let's look at the second line, shall we?"

The music teacher could not control her class. A deafening noise always came from her room. One day when it was worse than usual the English mistress could bear it no longer. She ran into the music room where she found the music teacher sitting at her piano and the boys and girls raising Cain.
"Do you know my pupils can't concentrate for the din in here?" the English teacher said.
"No!" said the music teacher. "But if you hum it I'll try and follow."

Why are some teachers jealous of driving instructors?
Because driving instructors are allowed to belt their pupils.

The headmaster was interviewing a new teacher. "You'll get $10,000 to start, with $15,000 after six months." "Oh!" said the teacher. "I'll come back in six months then."

"What do you do?" a man asked a very attractive girl at a party.
"I'm an infant teacher."
"Good gracious! I thought you were at least twenty-six."

Why is a man wearing sunglasses like a rotten teacher?
Because he keeps his pupils in the dark.

A teacher in a country school received the following letter from one his student's mothers:
"Dear Teacher,
Please excuse Phil from school last week. His father was ill and the pig had to be fed."

Why are art galleries like retirement homes for teachers?
Because they're both full of old masters.

It was sweltering hot outside. The teacher came into the classroom wiping his brow and said, "Ninety-two today. Ninety-two."
"Happy birthday to you. Happy birthday to you. . ." sang the class.

Did you hear about the brilliant geography master?
He had abroad knowledge of his subject.

At a very upper-class school the girls were discussing their family pets.
"We've got a beautiful spaniel at our place," said one girl.
"Does it have a pedigree?" asked another.
"It does on its mother's side. And its father comes from a very good neighborhood."

"Jim won't be at school today," said his mother on the telephone. "He's broken an arm."
"Well tell him we hope he gets better soon."
"Oh he's fine now," said the mother. "It was my arm he broke."

Two little girls at a very posh school were talking to each other.
"I told the chauffeur to take his peaked cap off in case the other girls here thought I was a snob," said the first.
"How strange," said the second. "I told mine to keep his on in case anyone thought he was my father."

Unfortunately the secretary made a typing mistake in a circular letter to the parents and announced that the fees were to be increased by $500 per *anus* instead of *annum*.

"Jim," said his father when he read the letter. "I'm taking you away from that school. No son of mine is going to be educated with a lot of bums."

Miss Simons agreed to be interviewed by Jim for the school magazine.

"How old are you, Miss?" asked Jim.

"I'm not going to tell you that."

"But Mr Hill the technical teacher and Mr Hill the geography teacher told me how old they were."

"Oh well," said Miss Simons. "I'm the same age as both of them."

The poor teacher was not happy when she saw what Jim wrote:

"Miss Simons, our English teacher, confided in me that she was as old as the Hills."

The schoolteacher was furious when Jim knocked him down with his new bicycle in the playground.

"Don't you know how to ride that yet?" he roared.

"Oh yes!" shouted Jim over his shoulder. "It's the bell I can't work yet."

Mouse I: "I've trained that crazy science teacher at last."

Mouse II: "How have you done that?"

Mouse I: "I don't know how, but everytime I run through that maze and ring the bell, he gives me a piece of cheese."

"What's your father's occupation?" asked the school secretary on the first day of the new term.

"He's a conjurer, Miss," said the new boy.

"How interesting. What's his favorite trick?"

"He saws people in half."

"Golly! Now next question. Any brothers and sisters?"

"One half-brother and two half-sisters."

Billy's mother was called into the school one day by the principal.

"We're very worried about Billy," he said. "He goes round all day 'cluck, cluck, clucking.' "

"That's right," said Billy's mother.

"He thinks he's a chicken."

"Haven't you taken him to a psychiatrist?"

"Well we would, but we need the eggs."

Two elderly teachers were talking over old times and saying how much things had changed. "I mean," said the first, "I caught one of the boys kissing one of the girls yesterday."

"Extraordinary," said the second. "I didn't even kiss my wife before I married her, did you?"

"I can't remember. What was her maiden name?"

"Please Sir. There's something wrong with my stomach."

"Well button up your jacket and no one will notice."

"Now remember, boys and girls," said the science teacher, "you can tell a tree's age by counting the rings in a cross section. One ring for each year."

Alec went home for tea and found a Swiss Roll on the table.

"I'm not eating that, Mom," he said. "It's five years old."

A warning to any young sinner,
Be you fat or perhaps even thinner.
If you do not repent,
To Hell you'll be sent.
With nothing to eat but school dinner.

Why did the science teacher marry the school cleaner?
Because she swept him off his feet.

A mother was desperate to get her under-age daughter into kindergarten and was trying to impress the headmistress with the child's intellectual abilities. "She'll easily keep up with the others even though she is a year younger."
"Well," said the teacher doubtfully. "Could she prove it by saying something?"
"Certainly Miss," said the child. "Something pertaining to your conversation, or something purely irrelevant?"

"Did you know that eight out of ten schoolchildren use ballpoint pens to write with?"
"Gosh! What do the other two use them for?"

Why did the flea fail his exams?
He wasn't up to scratch.

"I asked you to draw a pony and trap," said the art master. "You've only drawn the pony. Why?"
"Well, Sir, I thought the pony would draw the trap."

On the first day at school the children were sizing each other up and boasting, trying to make good impressions on each other.
"I come from a one-parent family," said one little girl proudly.
"That's nothing. Both my parents remarried after they got divorced. I come from a four-parent family."

Do you know that if you laid all the economics teachers in the world end to end you'd still not come to a definite conclusion?

"You never get anything right," complained the teacher. "What kind of job do you think you'll get when you leave school?"
"Well I want to be the weather girl on TV."

"Why have you written that Shakespeare was a corset manufacturer before he became a playwright?" asked the English teacher.
"Because he wrote that he could put a girdle round the earth in 40 minutes."

Why did the school cleaner take early retirement?
Because he realized that grime doesn't pay.

What subject are witches good at in school?
English! Because they're the tops at spelling.

"What shall we play today?" said Theresa to her best
friend Emma.
"Let's play schools," said Emma.
"OK!" said Theresa. "But I'm going to be absent."

"Now don't forget, boys," said the science teacher with
a strange sense of logic. "If it wasn't for water we
would never learn to swim. And if we'd never learned
to swim, just think how many people would have
drowned!"

Mr Jones, the art teacher, was very small and very
meek. One day he found his car smeared with rude
words painted bright red.
He told the principal who told the school that unless
someone owned up the half-term holiday would be
cancelled.
A few minutes after assembly there was a knocking on
Mr Jones's door. "Come in!" he called and there was
Nigel Hawkins, the school bully – six feet tall and built
like a tank.
"It was me what painted the words on your car."
"Oh thank you for confessing," gulped Mr Jones. "I'm
not sure that your spelling was 100 per cent accurate,
but I thought you'd like to know that I loved the color."

The teacher glanced up at the clock and then checked the time with his watch. "That clock's fast," he told the class.

"I hope so, Sir. If it isn't, it'll fall down and break."

"Your pupils must miss you a lot," said the woman in the next bed to the teacher in hospital.

"Not at all! Their aim's usually good. That's why I'm here."

"I did not come into the classroom to listen to you lot being impertinent," complained the teacher.

"Oh! Where do you usually go, Miss?"

At graduation day to mark the end of a particularly trying year the principal said, "A parent said to me recently that half the teachers do all the work and the other half nothing at all. I'd like to assure all the parents here this afternoon that at this school the opposite is the case."

At the school concert, Wee Willie had volunteered to play his bagpipes. The noise was dreadful, like a choir of cats singing off-key. After he'd blown his way through *The Flowers of the Forest* he said, "Is there anything you'd like me to play?"

"Yes!" cried a voice from the back of the hall. "Dominoes!"

"I've lost my Dad," a little boy wailed at the school gate after everyone else had gone home.

"Never mind," said the teacher. "What's he like?"

" 'Wine women and song' according to Mommy."

A teacher was correcting exam papers when he came across Alec's effort: a sheet of paper, blank apart from his name and "Act II Macbeth. Scene V. Line 28." The teacher reached for his Shakespeare and turned to Macbeth where he found that the 28th line of the fifth scene of the second act read, "I cannot do this bloody thing."

"How do you spell 'blancmange'?" the dinner lady asked her assistant when she was chalking up the lunch menu.

"Er . . . b.l.a.m . . . no . . . er, b.l.a.a . . . no . . ."

"Never mind," said the dinner lady. "Tony," she shouted to the other assistant. "Open a tin of rice pudding will you?"

"I'm not going to school today," Alexander said to his mother. "The teachers bully me and the boys in my class don't like me."

"You're going. And that's final. I'll give you two good reasons why."

"Why?"

"Firstly, you're 35 years old. Secondly, you're the principal."

"Please, Miss! How do you spell 'ichael'?"

The teacher was rather bewildered. "Don't you mean Michael?"

"No Miss. I've written the 'M' already."

"What did the doctor say to you yesterday?" asked the teacher.

"He said I was allergic to horses."

"I've never heard of anyone suffering from that. What's the condition called?"

"Bronco-itis."

"I want you to help me stop my son gambling," an anxious father said to his boy's principal. "I don't know where he gets it from but it's bet, bet, bet."

"Leave it to me," said the principal.

A week later he phoned the boy's father. "I think I've cured him," he said.

"How?"

"Well, I saw him looking at my beard and he said, 'I bet that's a false beard.' 'How much?' I said. And he said, '$5.'"

"What happened?" asked the father.

"Well, he tugged my beard which is quite natural and I made him give me $5. I'm sure that'll teach him a lesson."

"No it won't," said the father. "He bet me $10 this morning that he'd pull your beard with your permission by the end of the week."

"I have decided to abolish all corporal punishment at this school," said the principal at morning assembly. "That means that there will be no physical punishment."

"Does that mean that you're stopping school dinners as well, Sir?"

Teacher's strong; teacher's gentle.
Teacher's kind. And I am mental.

"Please Sir! Please Sir! Why do you keep me locked up in this cage?"
"Because you're the teacher's pet."

"Why don't you like this country?" the teacher asked a Californian boy who had come to school.
"It's the weather," drawled Bud. "I'm not used to the rain. At home we have 365 days of sunshine every year – at least."

"Ann!" the teacher shouted one day at the girl who had been daydreaming out the window. "If India has the world's second largest population: oranges are 50 cents for six: and it costs $3 for a day return to Austin: how old am I?"
"32!"
"Why did you say that?"
Well, my brother's 16 and he's half mad!"

What did the bookworm say to the school librarian?
"Can I burrow this book please?"

"Miss Stephens took us to the zoo today, Mom."
"What did you see?"
"There were lions, tigers, elephants; oh, and gnus that were in two separate pens."
"Why are they separated?"
"Because there's good gnus and there's bad gnus."

A gym teacher who came from Quebec,
Wrapped both legs around his neck.
But sad, he forgot
How to untie the knot
And now he's a highly-strung wreck.

The teacher was furious with her son. "Just because
you've been put in my class, there's no need to think
you can take liberties. You're a pig."
The boy said nothing.
"Well! Do you know what a pig is?"
"Yes Mom," said the boy. "The offspring of a swine."

A teacher caught one of her students stealing apples.
The lad stood in front of her trying to hide the apples
behind his back.
"What's your name again?" asked the teacher.
"Leo."
"And whose class are you in?"
"Mr Scorpio's."
"And where do you live?"
"Capricorn Street."
"And what are you hiding behind your back?"
"Nothing, Miss. Honest."

Why did the teacher have her hair in a bun?
Because she had her nose in a hamburger.

"I was doing my homework yesterday and I asked my
dad what a circle is. He said it's a round straight line
with a hole in the middle."

Why is the stupid red-headed boy like a biscuit?
Because he's a ginger nut.

How do you keep a stupid person happy for hours?
Give him a piece of paper with PTO written on both
sides.

It's obvious that animals are smarter than humans. Put
eight horses in a race and 20,000 people will go along
to see it. But put eight people in a race and not one
horse will bother to go along and watch.

Jane's father decided to take all the family out to a
restaurant for a meal. As he'd spent quite a lot of
money for the meal he said to the waiter, "Could I have
a bag to take the leftovers home for the dog?"
"Gosh!" exclaimed Jane, "Are we getting a dog?"

A fat girl went into a cafe and ordered two slices of
apple pie with four scoops of ice cream covered with
lashings of raspberry sauce and piles of chopped nuts.
"Would you like a cherry on the top?" asked the
waitress.
"No, thanks," said the girl, "I'm on a diet."

One day Bob's mother turned to Bob's father and said, "It's such a nice day, I think I'll take Bob to the zoo." "I wouldn't bother," said father, "If they want him, let them come and get him."

Why is it that when I stand on my head the blood rushes to my head but when I stand on my feet the blood doesn't rush to my feet?
You're feet aren't empty.

A woman telephoned her local newspaper to let them know that she had just given birth to 18 children. The reporter didn't quite hear the message and said, "Would you repeat that?"
"Not if I can help it," replied the woman.

Why did the stupid person give up his attempt to cross the Channel on a plank?
He couldn't find a plank that was long enough.

Beautician: "Did that mud pack I gave you for your wife improve her appearance?"
Man: "It did for a while – then it fell off."

"Our librarian is so stupid she thinks that an autobiography is a book about the life story of a car."

Eddy's father called up to him: "Eddy, if you don't stop playing that trumpet I think I'll go crazy."
"I think you are already," replied Eddy "I stopped playing half an hour ago."

Did you hear about the man who hijacked a submarine?
He demanded a million dollars and a parachute.

When he received the end of term report Brenda's father went crazy. "This report is terrible," he said, "I'm not at all pleased with it."
"I told the teacher you wouldn't like it," said Brenda, "But he insisted on sending it just the same."

What is black, gushes out of the ground and shouts "Excuse me"?
Refined oil.

A stupid glazier was examining a broken window. He looked at it for a while and then said: "It's worse than I thought. It's broken on both sides."

Roger is so lazy that when he drops something he waits till he has to tie his shoelaces before he'll pick it up.

Why do stupid people eat biscuits?
Because they're crackers.

Why did the robot act stupid?
Because he had a screw loose.

My sister is so dim she thinks that a cartoon is a song you sing in a car.

The garbage men were just about to leave the street when a woman came running out of the house carrying some cardboard boxes.
"Am I too late for the garbage?" she called. "No, lady," replied one of the men, "Jump right in!"

When my girlfriend goes out riding, she looks like part of the horse. When she dismounts, she still looks like part of the horse.

Joan's teacher got so fed up of her fooling around in class that he wrote a letter of complaint to her father.
"What's all this about?" roared Dad, "Your teacher says he finds it impossible to teach you anything."
"I told you he was no good," said Joan.

Jim: "Our dog is just like one of the family."
Fred: "Which one?"

Did you hear about the florist who had two children? One's a budding genius and the other's a blooming idiot.

Neil: "I've changed my mind."
Jim: "About time, too. Does the new one work any better?"

Girl: "Did you like that cake, Mrs Jones?"
Mrs Jones: "Yes, very much."
Girl: "That's funny. My mum said you didn't have any taste."

Did you hear about the man who tried to iron his curtains? He fell out of the window.

"My wife has a slight impediment in her speech. Every so often, she has to stop to breathe."

A woman woke her husband in the middle of the night.
"There's a burglar downstairs eating the cake that I made this morning."
"Who shall I call," her husband said, "Police or ambulance?"

"My mother is so stupid that she thinks a string quartet is four people playing tennis."

A man telephoned London Airport. "How long does it take to get to New York?"
"Just a minute."
"Thanks very much."

"This morning I felt that today was going to be my lucky day. I got up at seven, had seven dollars in my pocket, there were seven of us at lunch and there were seven horses in the seven o'clock race – so I backed the seventh."
"Did it win?"
"No, it came seventh."

"You should get a job in the meteorology office."
"Why?"
"Because you're an expert on wind."

"That boy is so dirty, the only time he washes his ears is when he eats watermelon."

"My grandad has so many wrinkles he has to screw his hat on."

Fred: "I was sorry to hear that your mother-in-law had died. What was the complaint?"
Ted: "We haven't had any yet."

"My friend is so stupid that he thinks twice before saying nothing."

Why did the stupid sailor grab a bar of soap when his ship sank?
He thought he could wash himself ashore.

An irate woman burst into the baker's shop and said:
"I sent my son in for two pounds of biscuits this morning but when I weighed them there was only one pound. I suggest you check your scales."
The baker looked at her calmly for a moment or two and then replied: "Madam, I suggest you weigh your son."

"Waiter, how long have you worked here?"
"Six months, sir."
"Well, it can't have been you who took my order."

"Did you hear about the sailor that was discharged from the submarine service? – He was caught sleeping with the windows open."

"We had sponge cake for tea yesterday. Mom sponged the flour from the woman next door ... the milk from our landlady ... and one dollar for the gas from the traveling salesman."

"My dad thinks he wears the trousers in our house – but it's always mum who tells him which pair to put on."

At the inquest into her husband's death by food poisoning Mrs Wally was asked by the coroner if she could remember her husband's last words. "Yes," she replied." He said "I don't know how that shop can make a profit from selling this salmon at only 20 cents a tin...."

"When you leave school, you should become a bone specialist. You've certainly got the head for it."

An idiotic laborer was told by an equally idiotic foreman to dig a hole in the road.
"And what shall I do with the earth, sir?" asked the laborer.
"Don't be daft, man," he replied. "Just dig another hole and bury it."

Did you hear about the stupid motorist who always drove his car in reverse? It was because he knew the town backward."

What's the most important thing to remember in Chemistry?
Never lick the spoon.

"Look at that bald man over there. It's the first time I've seen a parting with ears."

Two shark fishermen were sitting on the side of their boat just off the coast of Florida, cooling their feet in the sea. Suddenly an enormous shark swam up and bit off one fisherman's leg.
"A shark's just bitten off my leg," yelled the fisherman.
"Which one?" asked his friend.
"I don't know, replied the first, "When you've seen one shark, you've seen them all."

"My auntie Maud had so many candles on her last birthday cake that all her party guests got sunburnt."

A woodpecker was pecking a hole in a tree. All of a sudden a flash of lightning struck the tree to the ground. The woodpecker looked bemused for a moment and then said: "Gee, I guess I don't know my own strength."

There's a large crack in the sitting room of Jimmy's house so he goes around telling everyone that he's from a broken home.

What happened to the man who couldn't tell the difference between porridge and putty?
All his windows fell out.

A stupid bank robber rushed into a bank, pointed two fingers at the clerk and said: "This is a muck up."
Don't you mean a stick up?" asked the girl.
"No," said the robber, "it's a muck up. I've forgotten my gun."

When Wally Witherspoon proposed to his girlfriend she said:
"I love the simple things in life, Wally, but I don't want one of them for a husband."

"I beg your pardon," said the man, returning to his seat in the theater, "But did I step on your toe as I went out?"
"You certainly did," the woman replied.
"Oh good," said the man, "that means I'm in the right row."

Psychiatrist: "Well, what's your problem?"
Patient: "I prefer brown shoes to black shoes."
Psychiatrist: "There's nothing wrong with that. Lots of people prefer brown shoes to black shoes. I do myself."
Patient: "Really? How do you like yours – fried or boiled?"

"At our local restaurant you can eat dirt cheap – but who wants to eat dirt?"

A policeman was amazed to see a hiker walking along the road carrying a signpost which read "To Brighton."
"Allo, allo, allo," said the policeman, "What are you doing with that?"
"I'm walking to Brighton," said the hiker, "And I don't want to lose my way."

Did you hear about the dizzy boy scout?
He spent all day doing good turns.

"Can you stand on your head?"
"I've tried, but I can't get my feet up high enough."

How do you confuse an idiot?
Give him two spades and ask him to take his pick.

A stupid man spent the evening with some friends, but when the time came for him to leave, a terrific storm started with thunder, lightning and torrential rain. "You can't go home in this," said the host, "you'd better stay the night."
"That's very kind of you," said the man, "I'll just pop home and get my pajamas."

A boy went into a cafe and ordered a can of lemonade. He took a can opener from his pocket, opened the can and drank the lemonade. The girl behind the counter asked why he didn't use the ring pull to open the can and he replied, "Oh, I thought that was only for people who didn't have a can opener with them."

Knock! Knock!
Who's there?
Armageddon.
Armageddon who?
Armageddon out of here!

Dave: "What did you have for supper?"
Mave: "It was what I call an Eastern Mediterranean dish."
Dave: "What do you mean?"
Mave: "Full of Greece."

"What should you do if you swallow a lightbulb?"
"Spit it out and be delighted!"

Did you hear about the millionaire who had a bad accident?
He fell off his wallet.

A man who was very upset walked in to see his doctor.
"Doctor, you've got to help me!" he wailed.
"What seems to be the trouble?" asked the doctor.
"I keep having the same dream, night after night.
There's this door with a sign on it, and I push and push the door but I can't get it open."
"What does the sign on the door say?" asked the doctor.
"Pull," said the patient.

What happened to Lady Godiva's horse when he realized that she wasn't wearing any clothes?
It made him shy.

A mountaineer fell down a very deep crevasse, breaking both his arms. Another member of the party managed to lower a rope until it was just within reach of the man's head.
"Quick!" he shouted. "Get hold of the rope with your teeth and I'll pull you up." Inch by painful inch, the mountaineer was dragged back up the crevasse.
When he only had two feet to go, his rescuer called out, "Are you all right?"
"Yes, aaaaaaaaarrrrrrrrgggggghhhhhh!" came the reply.

On Fred's 17th birthday, his Dad said he'd take him out for his first driving lesson. As they got in the car, the father said, "Just one thing, Fred. If you're going to hit anything, make sure it's cheap."

A doctor visited his patient in the hospital ward after the operation. "I've got some bad news – we amputated the wrong leg. Now the good news – the man in the next bed wants to buy your slippers."

A woman was in court charged with wounding her husband. "But madam, why did you stab him over 100 times?" asked the judge.
"Oh, your Honor," replied the defendant, "I didn't know how to switch off the electric carving knife."

There was once a puppy called May who loved to pick quarrels with animals who were bigger than she was. One day she argued with a lion. The next day was the first of June.
Why? Because that was the end of May!

"Doctor, doctor, I think I'm a spoon."
"Sit over there, please, and don't stir."

"What kind of cats love water?"
"Octopusses."

Two friends were discussing the latest scandalous revelations about a Hollywood actress.
"They say she likes her latest husband so much she's decided to keep him for another month," said one to the other.

Uncle Hubert noticed that his nephew Johnny was watching him the whole time.
"Why are you always looking at me?" he asked.
"I was just wondering when you were going to do your trick," replied Johnny.
"What trick?" enquired Uncle Hubert.
"Well, Mom and Dad say you drink like a fish."

"What do you get if you cross a hedgehog with a giraffe?"
"A long-necked toothbrush."

Two beings from outer space landed in Las Vegas and were wandering around the casinos. One of them volunteered to go inside and see what was happening. He came out looking rather shocked. "What's the matter?" asked his friend.
"It's a very popular place," replied the first being. "It's full of creatures that keep vomiting up little metal disks."

"Doctor, doctor, my son's just swallowed some gunpowder!"
"Well, don't point him at me."

"Doctor, doctor, I'm at death's door!"
"Don't worry, Mrs Jenkins. An operation will soon pull you through."

"Doctor, doctor, Cuthbert keeps biting his nails!"
"That's not serious in a child."
"But Cuthbert bites his toe nails."

What do Paddington Bear and Winnie the Pooh pack for their holidays?
The bear essentials.

Tim once took his small cousin with him while he went fishing. When he returned, he was looking very fed up.
"I'll never do that again," he complained to his Dad.
"Did she frighten off the fish?" enquired Dad.
"No," replied Tim. "She sat on the bank and ate all my maggots."

Britain's oldest lady was 115 years old today, and she hasn't got a gray hair on her head. She's completely bald.

Doctor: "Good morning, Mrs Feather. Haven't seen you for a long time."
Mrs Feather: "I know, doctor. It's because I've been ill."

Doctor: "Come over to the window, Mr Ample, and stick out your tongue."
Mr Ample: "Do you want to have a good look at it, doctor?"
Doctor: "No, but I want to pay my neighbors back for their son's rudeness."

Why do vampires never get fat?
They eat necks to nothing.

What does a headless horseman ride?
A nightmare.

Why did the farmer plow his field with a steamroller?
Because he planned to grow mashed potatoes.

What happens when a band plays in a thunderstorm?
The conductor gets hit by lightning.

"Doctor, doctor, I think I'm Napoleon."
"How long have you felt like this?"
"Ever since Waterloo."

"What sort of sentence would you get if you broke the
law of gravity?"
"A suspended one."

"What's the best place to find diamonds?"
"In a pack of cards."

On Sam's first day at school, the teacher was telling
the class about all the different sorts of birds, and their
various habits. She asked the class if anyone knew the
names of the birds which didn't build their own nests.
Sam stuck his hand in the air and said, "The cuckoo,
Miss."
"Very good, Sam," said the teacher. "How did you
know that?"
"Oh, Miss, everyone knows that cuckoos live in
clocks!"

Doctor: "And did you drink your medicine after your bath, Mrs Soap?"
Mrs Soap: "No, doctor. By the time I'd drunk the bath there wasn't room for medicine."

"Doctor, I keep stealing things. What can I do?"
"Try to resist the temptation, but if you can't, get me a new television."

Why does a stork stand on one leg?
Because it would fall over if it lifted the other one.

Sally: "Our teacher has what is called a sympathetic face."
Wally: "What do you mean?"
Sally: "People look at her and feel sympathetic."

What do you get if you cross a bumble bee with a doorbell?
A humdinger.

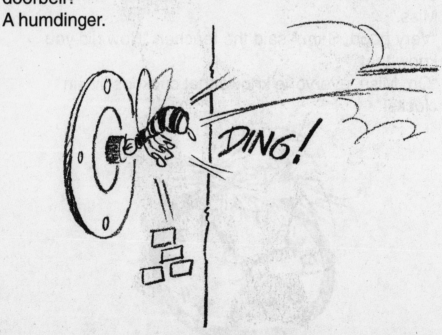

What's large and green and sits in a corner on its own all day?
The Incredible Sulk.

"Waiter, waiter, this lobster's only got one claw."
"It must have been in a fight, sir."
"Then bring me the winner."

Flash Harry gave his girlfriend a mink stole for his birthday. Well, it may not have been mink, but it's fairly certain it was stole.

Nicky and Vicky were talking about a famous, very glamorous film star. "What do you think of her clothes?" asked Nicky.
"I'd say they were chosen to bring out the bust in her," replied Vicky.

What's white and flies?
Super Spud.

How did the baker get an electric shock?
He stood on a bun and a current ran up his leg.

Did you hear about Lenny the Loafer? He is so lazy
that he sticks his nose out of the window so that the
wind will blow it for him.

Are vampires mad?
Well, they're often bats.

First flea: "You don't look too well."
Second flea: "I'm not really feeling up to scratch."

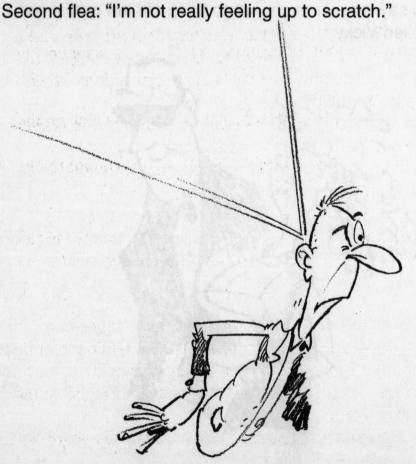

What sort of ship does Count Dracula sail on?
A blood vessel.

"Doctor, doctor, how can I stop my cold going to my chest?"
"Tie a knot in your neck."

"Do you always talk like that or are you wearing itchy underwear?"

"My sister is so stupid she thinks that aroma is someone who travels a lot."

"Did you hear about the idiot who won the Tour de France?"
"He did a lap of honor."

"What fish tastes best with cream?"
"A jellyfish."

"When I was at school I was as smart as the next fellow. What a pity the next fellow was such an idiot."

"I didn't recognize you for a minute. It was one of the happiest minutes of my life."

One day Tony's girlfriend wrote to him to say their friendship was off and could she have her photograph back.
Tony sent her a pile of pictures of different girls with the message, "I can't remember what you look like. Could you please take out your photo and return the rest?"

The great Roman emperor Nero was watching Christians being thrown to the lions.
"One good thing about this sport," he said to one of his aides, "We're never bothered with spectators running onto the pitch."

"She's such a gossip it doesn't take her long to turn an earful into a mouthful."

"Mom and dad are in the iron and steel business. She does the ironing and he does the stealing."

"My friend is so stupid he thinks that an autograph is a chart showing sales figures for cars."

Did you hear about the idiotic goalkeeper who saved a penalty but let it in on the action replay?

"My dog saw a sign that said: 'Wet Paint' – so he did!"

Why did the idiots' tug o' war team lose the match?
They pushed.

"My dad is a real jerk. I told him I needed an encyclopedia for school and he said I'd have to walk just like everyone else!"

What's a porcupine's favorite food?
Prickled onions.

An idiot decided to start a chicken farm so he bought a hundred chickens to start. A month later he returned to the dealer for another hundred chickens because all of the first lot had died. A month later he was back at the dealers for another hundred chickens for the second lot had also died. "But I think I know where I'm going wrong," said the idiot, "I think I'm planting them too deep."

Modern music isn't as bad as it sounds.

"Claire's singing is improving. People are putting cotton wool in only one ear now."

A garbage man was walking along whistling while balancing a bin on his head and one on each shoulder. "How do you manage to do that?" asked Jane. "It's easy," replied the dustman, "Just put your lips together and blow."

Roger was in a very full bus when a fat woman opposite said, "If you were a gentleman, young man, you'd stand up and let someone else sit down." "And if you were a lady," replied Roger, "You'd stand up and let four people sit down."

"Doctor, doctor, I keep losing my memory." "When did you first notice that?" "When did I first notice what?"

Teacher: "If you add 20,567 to 23,678 and then divide by 97 what do you get?"
Jim: "The wrong answer."

Young Actor: "Dad, guess what? I've just got my first part in a play. I play the part of a man who's been married for 30 years."
Father: "Well, keep at it, son. Maybe one day you'll get a speaking part."

The plumber was working in a house when the lady of the house said to him: "Will it be alright if I have a bath while you're having your lunch?"
"It's okay with me, lady," said the plumber, "As long as you don't splash my sandwiches."

Salesman: "This spray is guaranteed to kill every single germ in the house."
Housewife: "What about the married ones?"

Thought for the day: Where do fathers learn all the things they tell their sons not to do?

"My dog is a nuisance. He chases everyone on a bicycle. What can I do?"
"Take his bike away."

"Last night I wrote myself a letter. But I forgot to sign it and now I don't know who it's from."

"We're so poor that Mom and Dad can't afford to buy me shoes. I have to blacken my feet and lace my toes together."

"Doctor, doctor, my left leg is giving me a lot of pain."
"I expect that's old age."
"But my right leg is as old, and that doesn't hurt at all!"

Why do surgeons wear masks in the operating theater?
So that if they make a mistake no one will know who did it.

What's thick, black, floats on water and shouts "Knickers!"?
Crude oil.

There was once a man who always went to work on an egg. One morning it wouldn't start, so he phoned the Automobile Association. They told him to pull out the yolk. He did, and the egg started. When he got to work he phoned the Automobile Association to thank them for their help and tell them his egg was all white now.

"Little Miss Muffet
Sat on a tuffet
Eating a bowl of stew
Along came a spider
And sat down beside her.
Guess what? She ate him up too!"

Did you hear about the stupid Australian who received a new boomerang for his birthday? He spent two days trying to throw the old one away.

"My son's just received a scholarship to medical school – but they don't want him while he's alive."

The seaside resort we went to last year was so boring that one day the tide went out and never came back.

What's an American cat's favorite car?
A Catillac.

"My big brother is such an idiot. The other day I saw him hitting himself on the head with a hammer. He was trying to make his head swell so his hat wouldn't fall over his eyes."

"My Mother uses lemon juice for her complexion. Maybe that is why she always looks so sour."

Where is the dead center of Boston?
The cemetery.

What's black and white and makes a lot of noise?
A zebra with a set of drums.

As he was walking along the street the vicar saw a little girl trying to reach a high door knocker. Anxious to help, the vicar went over to her. "Let me do it, dear," he said, rapping the knocker vigorously. "Great!" said the girl, "Now run like hell."

My auntie Mabel has got so many double chins it looks like she is peering over a pile of crumpets.

A man went into the local department store where he saw a sign on the escalator – "Dogs must be carried on this escalator." The silly man then spent the next two hours looking for a dog.

When doing exams Dick knows all the answers. It's the questions that get him confused.

"My sister is so dumb, she thinks that a buttress is a female goat."

Chuck: "Do you have holes in your underpants?"
Teacher: "No, of course not."
Chuck: "Then how do you get your feet through?"

How does an idiot call for his dog?
He puts two fingers in his mouth and then shouts
"Rover."

"My girlfriend talks so much that when she goes on
holiday, she has to spread suntan lotion on her
tongue."

"The hotel we stayed in for our holiday offered bed
and board, but it was impossible to say which was the
bed and which was the board."

What is a snail?
A slug with a crash helmet.

YEAH!

Did you hear about the idiotic karate champion who joined the army?
The first time he saluted, he nearly killed himself.

Did you hear about the idiot who made his chickens drink boiling water?
He thought they would lay hard boiled eggs.

Some people say the school cook's cooking is out of this world.
Most pupils wish it was out of their stomachs.

George is the type of boy that his mother doesn't want him to associate with!

At three o'clock one morning a veterinary surgeon was woken from a deep sleep by the ringing of his telephone. He staggered downstairs and answered the phone. "I'm sorry if I woke you," said a voice at the other end of the line.
"That's alright," said the vet, "I had to get up to answer the phone anyway."

Why was the musician arrested?
For getting into treble.

What's the difference between a bus driver and a cold in the head?
A bus driver knows the stops, and a cold in the head stops the nose.

"At my piano teacher's last performance the audience cheered and cheered. The piano was locked!"

Girl: "You think you're clever but really you're just stupid.
Her enemy: "You are like a piece of blotting paper. You soak everything in – but you get it all backwards!"

"Waiter, waiter, why is my apple pie all mashed up?"
"You did ask me to step on it, sir."

Boy Monster: "You've got a face like a million dollars."
Girl Monster: "Have I really?"
Boy Monster: "Yes – it's green and wrinkly."

Father: "There are 54 bars in Blackshoe and I'm proud to say that I've never been in one of them."
Mother: "Which one is that?"

A monster walked into a hamburger restaurant and ordered a cheeseburger, fries and a chocolate milkshake. When he finished his meal he left $10 to pay the bill. The waiter, thinking that the monster probably wasn't very good at adding up, gave him only 50 cents change.
At that moment another customer came in. "Gosh, I've never seen a monster in here before," he said.
"And you won't be seeing me again," said the monster furiously, "not at those prices."

A little boy came downstairs crying late one night. "What's wrong?" asked his mother. "Do people really come from dust, like they said in church?" he sobbed. "In a way they do," said his mother. "And when they die do they turn back to dust?" "Yes, they do." The little boy began to cry again. "Well, under my bed there's someone either coming or going."

What happened when the cows got out of their field? There was udder chaos.

1st Cannibal: "My dad's so tough he can kill crocodiles with his bare hands." 2nd Cannibal: "My dad's so tough it took six hours in the microwave to cook him."

"Would you say that a cannibal who ate his mother's sister was an aunt eater?"

A ghost was out haunting one night and met a fairy fluttering through the forest. "Hello," said the ghost. "I've never met a fairy before. What's your name?" "Nuff," said the fairy. "That's a very odd name," said the ghost. "No, it's not," said the fairy, offended, "haven't you heard of Fairy Nuff?"

A monster and a zombie went into the undertaker's.
"I'd like to order a coffin for a friend of mine who has
just died." said the monster.
"Certainly sir," said the undertaker, "but there was
really no need to bring him with you."

1st Werewolf: "Nerg."
2nd Werewolf: "Nerg, nerg, yug."
1st Werewolf: "Don't start changing the subject."

A monster went to see the doctor because he kept
bumping into things. "You need glasses," said the
doctor.
"Will I be able to read with them?" asked the monster.
"Yes."
"That's brilliant," said the monster. "I didn't know how
to read before."

The stupid monster went to the mind reader's and paid
$5 to have his thoughts read. After half an hour the
mind reader gave him his money back.

Why did the monster eat a lightbulb?
Because he was in need of light refreshment.

82

Knock, knock.
Who's there?
Francis.
Francis who?
Francis a country in Europe.

Cross-Eyed Monster: "When I grow up I want to be a bus driver."
Witch: "Well, I won't stand in your way."

Reports are coming in of an elephant running down the highway. Police ask motorists to drive carefully and to treat it as a roundabout.

What do you get if a huge hairy monster steps on Batman and Robin?
Flatman and Ribbon.

Did you hear about the girl monster who wasn't pretty and wasn't ugly?
She was pretty ugly.

What should you do if you find a gorilla sitting at your school desk?
Sit somewhere else.

What did the stupid ghost call his pet tiger?
Spot.

Did you hear about the stupid vampire who listened to a match?
He burned his ear!

Did you hear about the businessman who is so rich he has two swimming pools, one of which is always empty? It's for people who can't swim!

Why is twice ten the same as twice eleven?
Because twice ten is twenty, and twice eleven is twenty, too.

Did you hear about the short-sighted monster who fell in love with a piano? It had such wonderful white teeth, how could he resist it?

Did you hear about the bike that was possessed by devils and went around biting people?
It was known as a vicious cycle!

Teacher: "I see you don't cut your hair any longer."
Nigel: "No Sir, I cut it shorter."

Three travelers were crossing the bleak moors one night when a terrible storm blew up. Soaked to the skin and freezing, they made their way toward a dim light that flickered in the distance. When they reached it they discovered an eerie-looking house, with tall, twisted chimneys and hideous gargoyles leering down at them from the eaves. Despite their fears they knocked and the door was opened by an old crone wearing long black robes and with horrible warts all over her face.

"Come in, my dears," she smiled, revealing that most of her teeth were missing. " I had a feeling that you were coming."

Nervously the travelers entered the hall, which was full of purring black cats. A bat hung upside down from the lightbulb. "Can you put us up for the night?" stammered one of the men.

"Oh yes," said the witch. "But before I show you up to your beds, would you like a hot drink? Hot chocolate or coffee?"

"Hot chocolate for me, please." said the first man.

"Coffee for me, please," said the second man.

"I'll just have hot chocolate," said the third.

Which just goes to show that two out of three people prefer hot chocolate before they go to bed at night.

Did you hear about the competition to find the laziest spook in the world? All the competitors were lined up on stage. "I've got a really nice, easy job for the laziest person here," said the organizer. "Will the laziest spook raise his hand?"
All the spooks put up their hands -- except one.
"Why didn't you raise your hand?" asked the presenter.
"Too much trouble," yawned the spook!

A short, fat, hairy monster was waiting for a train and decided to while away the time by weighing himself on a machine on the station platform. Once he'd weighed himself he looked at the chart that indicated the ideal weight for each height.
"Having any problems?" asked another passenger.
"Are you overweight?"
"No," said the monster, "I'm just four feet too short."

Did you hear about the monster who ate bits of metal every night?
It was his staple diet.

The wizard who had invented a flying carpet was interviewed for a local radio station.
"What's it like, Merlin, to fly on a magic carpet?" asked the radio presenter.
"Rugged," replied Merlin.

Carol: "Our teacher gives me the pip."
Darryl: "What's her name?"
Carol: "Miss Lemmon."

A huge hairy monster went to the doctor to ask for help because he was becoming very weak. The doctor prescribed some pills and a tonic to build him up. A few days later the monster went back to the surgery.

"Are you feeling stronger?" asked the doctor.

"No," said the monster. "The medicine isn't working – you see, I can't get the lids off the bottles!"

If you're a regular at the Monster Cafe, you'll know that it isn't famous for either the quality or flavor of its food. Only the other day a vampire called the waiter over.

"Is this tea or coffee?" he asked. "It's disgusting – it tastes like disinfectant."

"In that case, it's tea," said the waiter. "Our coffee tastes like paraffin."

Did you hear about the absent-minded monster who went round and round in a revolving door for three hours?

He didn't know whether he was coming or going!

What do you call a monster with gravy, meat, and potatoes on his head?

Stew.

If a flying saucer is an aircraft, does that make a flying broomstick a witchcraft?

What did Tarzan say when he saw the monsters coming?
"Here come the monsters."
And what did he say when he saw the monsters coming with sunglasses on?
Nothing – he didn't recognize them!

What do you get if you cross a ghost with a packet of potato chips?
Snacks that go crunch in the night.

Why did Dr Frankenstein have his telephone cut off?
Because he wanted to win the Nobel prize!

What was Dr Jekell's favorite game?
Hyde and Seek.

"Waiter, waiter," called a diner at the Monster Cafe.
"There's a hand in my soup."
"That's not your soup, sir, that's your finger bowl."

Two monsters were working on building site. When lunchtime came, one of them took out a box of sandwiches. "Rat paste and tomato," he moaned, as he bit into the first. "More rat paste and tomato," he muttered as he ate the second.

"Rat paste and tomato?" his friend asked as he picked up the third sandwich.

"Yes," sighed the monster. "I hate rat paste and tomato."

"Why don't you ask your wife to make you something different?"

The monster looked at him strangely. " I don't have a wife – I make my sandwiches myself."

How does Dracula keep fit?
He plays batminton.

How do you get a ghost to lie perfectly flat?
You use a spirit level.

Alex and Alan took their lunches to the local cafe to eat.

"Hey!" shouted the proprietor. "You can't eat your own food in here!"

"Okay." said Alex. So he and Alan swapped their sandwiches.

Teacher: "Who can tell me what geese eat?"
Paul: "Er, gooseberries, Sir?"

Bob: "Our teacher is very musical you know."
Ben: "Musical? Mr Jenkinson?"
Bob: "Yes. He's always fiddling with his beard."

Science Teacher: "Can you tell me one substance that conducts electricity, Jane?"
Jane: "Why, er..."
Science Teacher: "Wire is correct."

Teacher: "Are you good at arithmetic?"
Mary: "Well, yes and no."
Teacher: "What do you mean, yes and no?"
Mary: "Yes, I'm no good at arithmetic."

Why is a classroom like an old car?
Because it's full of nuts, and has a crank at the front.

Why is a pencil the heaviest thing in your satchel?
Because it's full of lead.

The pupils in the 12th grade, who had learned to type, were being interviewed by prospective employers. Lisa was asked her typing speed.
"I'm not sure," she replied. "But I can rub out at 50 words a minute."

Teacher: "Dennis! When you yawn you should put your hand to your mouth."
Dennis: "What, and get it bitten?"

Alex's class went on a nature study ramble. "What do you call a thing with 10 legs, red spots and great big jaws, Sir?" asked Alex.
"I've no idea, why do you ask?" replied the teacher.
"Because one just crawled up your trouser leg."

Mrs Jones: "Well, Billy, how are you getting along with your trampolining lessons?"
Billy: "Oh, up and down, you know."

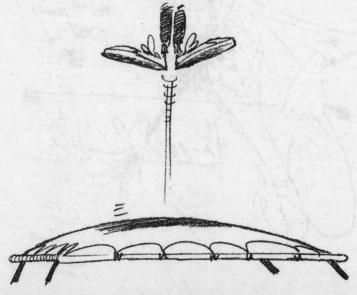

Mandy: "Our teacher went on a special banana diet."
Andy: "Did she lose weight?"
Mandy: "No, but she couldn't half climb trees well!"

Art Teacher: "What color would you paint the sun and the wind?"
Brian: "The sun rose, and the wind blue."

When is a blue school book not a blue school book?
When it is read.

When is an English teacher like a judge?
When she hands out long sentences.

Teacher: "Your books are a disgrace, Archibald. I don't see how anyone can possibly make as many mistakes in one day as you do."
Archibald: "I get here early, Sir."

Teacher: "Why do you want to work in a bank, Alan?"
Alan: " 'Cos there's money in it, Miss."

Biology Teacher: "What kinds of birds do we get in captivity?"
Janet: "Jail birds, Miss!"

Teacher: "Who was that on the phone, Samantha?"
Samantha: "No one important, Miss. Just some man who said it was long distance from Australia, so I told him I knew that already."

Teacher: "You're wearing a very strange pair of socks, Darren: One's blue with red spots, and one's yellow with green stripes."
Darren: "Yes, and I've got another pair just the same at home."

What game can you play with a shopping bag?
Basketball.

Teacher: "And did you see the Catskill Mountains on your visit to America?"
Jimmy: "No, but I saw them kill mice."

If a flying saucer is an aircraft, does that make a flying broomstick a witchcraft?

What were the only creatures not to go into the ark in pairs?
Maggots. They went in an apple.

Where can you dance in California?
San Fran-disco.

The class was set an essay on Shakespeare. Jacqui wrote in her book, "Shakespeare wrote tragedy, comedy, and errors."

Sandra's mother said no young man in his right mind would take her to the school dance in her bikini, so she decided to go with her friend's stupid brother.

Teacher: "Eat up your roast beef, it's full of iron."
Dottie: "No wonder it's so tough."

Mother: "Samantha! You came bottom out of 10 in arithmetic!"
Samantha: "Yes, Mom, but it could have been worse."
Mother: "How?"
Samantha: "I could have been in Sarah's group and come bottom out of 20."

Billy: "I thought there was a choice for dinner today."
Dinner Lady: "There is."
Billy: "No, there isn't. There's only cheese pie."
Dinner Lady: "You can choose to eat it or leave it."

What do you call a teacher floating on a raft in the sea?
Bob.

Two monsters were in hospital and they were discussing their operations and ailments. "Have you had your feet checked?" one asked the other. "No," came the reply. "They've always been purple with green spots."

A mother monster marched her naughty little monster into the doctor's surgery. "Is it possible that he could have taken his own tonsils out?" she asked.
"No," said the doctor.
"I told you so," said the mother monster. "Now, put them back."

What did the children do when there were rock cakes for lunch?
Took their pick.

Charlie: "Our school is so old I don't know what stops it from falling down."
Edward: "Maybe the woodworm hold hands."

Geography Teacher: "What mineral do we import from America?"
Daft Darren: "Coca Cola!"

Tommy was saying his prayers as his father passed by his bedroom door.

"God bless Mommy, and God bless Daddy, and please make Calais the capital of France."

"Tommy," said his father, "why do you want Calais to be the capital of France?"

"Because that's what I wrote in my geography test!"

What's black and white and horrible?
A math examination paper.

What did the dinner lady say when the teacher told her off for putting her finger in his soup? "It's all right, it isn't hot."

What do you call a ghost who only haunts the Town Hall?
The nightmayor.

How many vampires can you fit into an empty sports stadium?
One – after that it's not empty.

Monster: "Stick 'em down."
Ghost: "Don't you mean, stick 'em up?"
Monster: "No wonder I'm not making much money in this business."

What do you call a skeleton who goes out in the snow and rain without a coat or an umbrella?
A numbskull.

What did the werewolf eat after he'd had his teeth taken out?
The dentist.

Teacher: "You weren't at school last Friday, Robert. I heard you were out playing football."
Robert: "That's not true, Sir. And I've got the cinema tickets to prove it."

Andy: "What's the difference between a wage and a salary, Miss?"
Teacher: "If you earn a wage, you are paid every week, if you earn a salary, you are paid every month. Teachers, for example, get paid salaries because they are paid monthly."
Andy: "Please, Miss, where do they work?"

Monster: "I've got to walk 25 miles home."
Ghost: "Why don't you take a train?"
Monster: "I did once, but my mother made me give it back."

"I'm sorry to call you out at this time of night," said the witch, "but it's my poor black cat. He's just lying there telling me he wants to die."
The monster vet licked his lips. "Well, you've done the right thing by sending for me ..."

What happened when the ice monster had a furious row with the zombie?
He gave him the cold shoulder.

Which space movie stars Count Dracula?
The Vampire Strikes Back.

"Mommy, mommy, what's a vampire?"
"Be quiet, dear, and drink your soup before it clots."

Why don't ghosts make good magicians?
You can see right through their tricks.

Ghost: "Are you coming to my party?"
Spook: "Where is it?"
Ghost: "In the morgue – you know what they say, the morgue the merrier."

Dr Frankenstein: "Igor, have you seen my latest invention? It's a new pill consisting of 50 per cent glue and 50 per cent aspirin."
Igor: "But what's it for?"
Dr Frankenstein: "For monsters with splitting headaches."

Did you hear about the monster who went to a holiday camp? He won the ugly mug and knobbly knees competition and he wasn't even entered.

What did Frankenstein's monster say when he was struck by lightning?
"Thanks, I needed that."

Monster: "Please, help me, doctor. You see, I prefer jeans to tracksuits!"

Doctor: "That's not a problem. As a matter of fact, I prefer jeans to tracksuits too."

Monster: "What an incredible relief. And how do you like yours, doctor – boiled or roasted?"

1st Monster: "I'm so thirsty my tongue's hanging out."

2nd Monster: "Oh, I thought it was your tie!"

Why are monsters' fingers never more than 11 inches long?

Because if they were 12 inches, they would be a foot.

What did ET's mother say to him when he got home?

"Where on Earth have you been?"

What time is it when a monster sits on your car?

Time to get a new car.

How can you tell the difference between a monster and a banana?
Try picking it up. If you can't, it's either a monster or a giant banana.

Newsflash:
"Two monsters have escaped from prison today. One is orange and 9ft tall, and the other is green and yellow and 2ft 6in tall. The police are searching high and low for them."

A monster walked into the council rent office with a $5 note stuck in one ear and a $10 note in the other. You see, he was $15 in arrears.

What do you get if you cross a zombie with a boy scout?
A creature that scares old ladies across the road.

On her holidays, the geography teacher explained to the history teacher that she went to the Himalayas, visiting remote mountain areas. "In fact," she said, "we went where the hand of man has never set foot."

Teacher: "What is the longest night of the year?"
Alex: "A fortnight."

"Waiter, waiter, have you got frogs' legs?"
"No Sir, I always walk like this."

The games teacher had broken off her engagement.
The science teacher asked her what had happened. "I
thought it was love at first sight," said the science
teacher.
"It was, but it was the second and third sights that
changed my mind."

Teacher: "Recite your tables to me, Joan."
Joan: "Dining-room table, kitchen table, bedside
table....."

How did the teacher forecast the weather with a piece
of string?
She hung it up, and if it moved, she knew it was windy,
and if it got wet, she knew it was raining.

What should you do if you find yourself surrounded by Dracula, Frankenstein, a zombie and a werewolf? Hope you're at a fancy dress party.

Brian: "How did you manage to get a black eye?"
Bertie: "You see that tree in the playground?"
Brian: "Yes."
Bertie: "Well, I didn't."

Why did the teacher fix her bed to the chandelier?
Because she was a light sleeper.

What's the best way to avoid being troubled by biting insects?
Don't bite any!

At Christmas the school went to a special service in church. The teacher asked if they had enjoyed it, and if they had behaved themselves. "Oh yes, Miss," said Brenda. "A lady came round and offered us a plate full of money, but we all said no thank you."

Why did the headmaster stop wearing a flower in his buttonhole?
He got tired of the pot hitting his chest.

A school inspector was talking to a pupil. "How many teachers work in this school?" he asked.
"Only about half of them, I reckon," replied the pupil.

Two girls were talking in the corridor. "That boy over there is getting on my nerves," said Clarrie.
"But he's not even looking at you," replied Clara.
"That's what's getting on my nerves," retorted Clarrie.

Why should a school not be near a chicken farm?
To avoid the pupils overhearing fowl language.

Teacher: "What's the difference between a buffalo and a bison?"
Student: "You can't wash your hands in a buffalo, Miss."

Ben, sniffing: "Smells like UFO for dinner tonight, chaps."
Ken: "What's UFO?"
Ben: "Unidentified Frying Objects."

A motorist approached the principal one afternoon and said, "I'm awfully sorry, but I think I've just run over the school cat. Can I replace it?"
The principal looked him up and down and replied, "I doubt if you'd be the mouser she was."

Dave: "The trouble with our teachers is that they all do bird impressions."
Mave: "Really? What do they do?"
Dave: "They watch us like hawks."

Tracy: "Would you punish someone for something they haven't done?"
Teacher: "Of course not."
Tracy: "Oh good, because I haven't done my homework."

Teacher: "Martin, put some more water in the fish tank."
Martin: "But, Sir, they haven't drunk the water I gave them yesterday."

Teacher: "Andrew, your homework looks as if it is in your father's handwriting."
Andrew: "Well, I used his pen, Sir."

Father: "Would you like me to help you with your homework?"
Son: "No thanks, I'd rather get it wrong by myself."

1st Undertaker: "I've just been given the sack."
2nd Undertaker: "Why?"
1st Undertaker: "I buried someone in the wrong place."
2nd Undertaker: "That was a grave mistake."

What should you give short elves?
Elf-raising flour.

Statistics say that one in three people is mentally ill.
So check your friends and if two of them seem okay,
you're the one.

I wouldn't say our English teacher is fat, but when she got on a Speak Your Weight machine it surrendered.

A teacher went into a shoe shop. "I'd like some crocodile shoes, please," she said.
"Certainly, Madam," said the salesgirl. "How big is your crocodile?"

The young teacher was complaining to her friends about how badly she was being paid. "We get a really poultry amount each month," she said.
"You mean 'paltry'" corrected one of her friends.
"No I don't, I mean 'poultry'" replied the teacher. "What I earn is chicken feed."

Pupil to a dinner lady: "Excuse me, but I have a complaint."
Dinner lady: "This is the school dining-room, not the doctor's surgery."

A monster went to the doctor with a branch growing out of his head. "Hmm," said the doctor. "I've no idea what it is."

The next week the branch was covered in leaves and blossom. "I'm stumped," said the doctor, "but you can try taking these pills."

When the monster came back a month later the branch had grown into a tree, and just a few weeks later he developed a small pond, surrounded by trees and bushes, all of them on the top of his head.

"Ah!" said the doctor, "I know what it is. You've got a beauty spot!"

Why did the headmistress put wheels on her rocking chair?
She liked to rock and roll.

Why does the Hound of the Baskervilles turn round and round before he lies down for the night?
Because he's the watchdog and he has to wind himself up.

Piano Tuner: "I've come to tune the piano."
Music Teacher: "But we didn't send for you."
Piano Tuner: "No, but the people who live across the street did."

With whom does an elastic trumpet player play?
With a rubber band.

Did the bionic monster have a brother?
No, but he had lots of trans-sisters.

Good news – two boys went out one day climbing trees.
Bad news – one of them fell out.
Good news – there was a hammock beneath him.
Bad news – there was a rake beside the hammock.
Good news – he missed the rake.
Bad news – he missed the hammock too.

A man sat playing chess with a huge hairy purple monster in a pub. A stranger came in and sat down and in amazement watched them playing. When they had finished the game he came over. "I'm a movie producer," he explained as he introduced himself. "Your monster could make a fortune in Hollywood." The man just shrugged. "He's not that clever," he said dismissively, "I've just beaten him three times in the last four games."

What do you get if you cross a frog with a decathlete?
Someone who pole vaults without a pole.

The ghost teacher was giving her pupils instructions on how to haunt a house properly. "Has everyone got the hang of walking through walls?" she asked. One little ghoul at the front of the class looked uncertain. "Just watch the blackboard everyone," instructed the teacher, "and I'll go through it once more."

Did you hear about the Eskimo teacher who was reciting "Little Jack Horner" to her class of five-year-olds? She'd got as far as "Little Jack Horner sat in a corner" when one little girl put up her hand and said, "Please, Miss, what's a corner?"

Where does Dracula keep his savings? In the blood bank.

Why can't the deaf teacher be sent to prison? Because you can't condemn someone without a hearing.

Who wrote Count Dracula's life story? The ghost writer.

How can you drop an egg six feet without breaking it? By dropping it seven feet – it won't break for the first six.

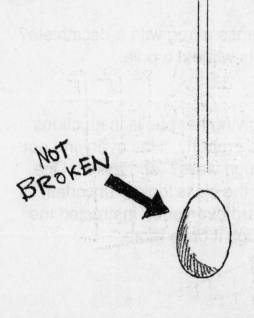

NOT BROKEN

Did you hear about the monster who was known as Captain Kirk?
He had a left ear, a right ear and a final front ear.

What did one of Frankenstein's ears say to the other?
I didn't know we were living on the same block.

"Mommy, mommy, teacher keeps saying I look like a werewolf."
"Be quiet dear and go and comb your face."

"Doctor, doctor, my wife thinks she's a duck."
"You better bring her in to see me straight away."
"I can't do that – she's already flown south for the winter."

What kind of beans do cannibals like best?
Human beans.

Why did Ken keep his trumpet in the fridge?
Because he liked cool music.

Why is school like a shower?
One wrong turn and you're in hot water.

Did you hear about the burglar who fell in the cement mixer?
Now he's a hardened criminal.

Why did the huge horrible monster go to see the psychiatrist?
Because he was worried that people liked him.

A monster went shopping with sponge-fingers in one ear and jelly and custard in the other.
"Why have you got jelly and custard sponge in your ears?" asked the shop assistant.
"You'll have to speak up," said the monster. "I'm a trifle deaf."

The principal was taking her class round an art gallery. She stopped in front of one exhibit, and sneered at the guide, "I suppose that is some kind of modern art?"

"No, madam," replied the guide. "I'm afraid it's a mirror."

Igor: "Only this morning Dr Frankenstein completed another amazing operation. He crossed an ostrich with a centipede."

Dracula: "And what did he get?"

Igor: "We don't know – we haven't managed to catch it yet."

Why did the monster jump up and down?

Because he'd just taken his medicine and he'd forgotten to shake the bottle.

Did you hear about the utterly brainless monster who sat on the floor? He fell off.

A monster decided to become a TV star, so he went to see an agent. "What do you do?" asked the agent.

"Bird impressions," said the monster.

"What kind of bird impressions?"

"I eat worms."

Did you hear about the skeleton which was attacked by the dog?
It ran off with some bones and left him without a leg to stand on.

Why did the monster take his nose apart?
To see what made it run.

Mary had a bionic cow,
It lived on safety pins.
And every time she milked that cow
The milk came out in tins.

A cannibal chief was just about to stew his latest victim for dinner when the man protested, "You can't eat me – I'm a manager!"
"Well," said the cannibal, "Soon you'll be a manager in chief."

What did the two acrobats say when they got married?
"We're head over heels in love!"

Why did the monster have to buy two tickets for the zoo?
One to get in and one to get out.

What do you get if you pour hot water down a rabbit hole?
Hot cross bunnies!

"Doctor, doctor, I've just swallowed the film from my camera."
"Well, let's hope nothing develops."

1st Monster: "That gorgeous four-eyed creature just rolled her eyes at me!"
2nd Monster: "Well, roll them back again – she might need them."

"Doctor, doctor, I think I'm invisible."
"Who said that?"

What's a cannibal's favorite game?
Swallow my leader.

On a coach trip to London a little girl kept sniffing.
"Haven't you got a hankie, dear?" asked a little old
lady across the aisle.
"Yes," replied the little girl. "But I'm not supposed to
talk to strangers, so I certainly can't lend you my
handkerchief."

What do you get if you cross a galaxy with a toad?
Star Warts.

On which side does a chicken have the most feathers?
On the outside.

Which bird is always out of breath? A puffin.

What's the best thing to give a seasick elephant?
Plenty of room.

Why was the mother kangaroo cross with her children?
Because they ate fries in bed.

Two friends who lived in the town were chatting. "I've just bought a pig," said the first.
"But where will you keep it?" said the second. "Your garden's much too small for a pig!"
"I'm going to keep it under my bed," replied his friend.
"But what about the smell?"
"He'll soon get used to that."

How does a Clever Dick spend hours on his homework every night, and yet get twelve hours sleep?
He puts his homework underneath his mattress.

Two neighbors were having a chat across the garden fence. "My son's learning to play American football," said one.
"Oh, really," said the other. "What position does he play?"
"The coach says he's a drawback."

What sort of fish performs surgical operations?
A sturgeon.

Did you hear about the two fat men who ran in the New York Marathon?
One ran in short bursts, the other in burst shorts!

What nickname did the police give to the new blonde woman police officer?
A fair cop.

How do we know that Rome was built at night?
Because all the books say it wasn't built in a day!

Did you hear about the dentist who became a brain surgeon?
His drill slipped.

What's the easiest way to make a banana split?
Cut it in half.

Which animals were the last to leave the ark?
The elephants – they were packing their trunks.

Did you hear about the schoolgirl who was so excited
about a book she found in the library called "How to
Hug"?
It turned out to be volume eight of an encyclopedia.

"Doctor, doctor, I'm really worried about my breathing."
"Don't be – we'll soon find something to stop it."

What is the most popular sentence at school?
I don't know.

Paul was staying with his grandparents, and one day he went up into the attic to play. Among all the old clothes, toys, and books, he found an old family Bible, which he took downstairs. As he opened it, a large pressed leaf fell to the floor. "Oh, look, Grandma," he said. "Adam left his clothes in the Bible."

And what goes into the water pink and comes out blue?
A swimmer on a cold day!

Just before the Ark set sail, Noah saw his two sons fishing over the side. "Go easy on the bait, lads," he said. "Remember I've only got two worms."

How can you see stars during the daytime?
Hit yourself on the head.

Ben's Dad was building a pine bookcase, and Ben was watching and occasionally helping. "What are the holes for?" Ben asked.
"They're knot holes," said his Dad.
"What are they, then, if they're not holes?" said Ben.

What do traffic control officers like for tea?
Traffic jam sandwiches.

Why do barbers make good drivers?
Because they know all the short cuts.

Did you hear about the two little boys who found
themselves in a modern art gallery by mistake?
"Quick," said one, "run! Before they say we did it!"

Did you hear about the idiot who had a new bath put
in? The plumber said, "Would you like a plug for it?"
The idiot replied, "Oh, I didn't know it was electric."

Wally Woollynut was given the job of painting a flagpole but he didn't know how much paint he would need. "Lay it down and measure it," suggested a friend.

"That's no good," said Wally, "I need to know the height, not the length."

Cannibal Boy: "I've brought a friend home for dinner."
Cannibal Mom: "Put him in the fridge and we'll have him tomorrow."

Did you hear that in the recent gales the fence blew down around the Pink and Pimply Nudist Camp?
A group of builders is looking into it.

Why did the teacher decide to become an electrician?
To get a bit of light relief.

What's a skeleton's favorite musical instrument?
A trombone.

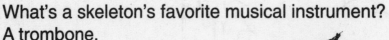

Tessa the toddler complained to her mother one evening, "Please can we have a new babysitter?"
"Why, Tessa," said her mother, "I thought you liked Barbara."
"I do," said Tessa. "But she tells me the same story every time she's here."
"Which story is that?" asked her mother.
"It's called 'Once Upon a Time.' And I know I've heard it before, so I go to sleep."

Why did JR see his lawyer?
Because he wanted to Sue Ellen.

What is a dimple?
A pimple going the wrong way.

What happened to the man who put his false teeth in backwards?
He ate himself!

Pupil: "Excuse me sir, but I don' t think I deserve a mark of zero for this exam paper."
Teacher: "Neither do I, but it's the lowest mark I can give."

What's a twip?
What a wabbit calls a twain ride!

What happened to the tailor who made his trousers
from sun-blind material?
Every time the sun came out, the trousers rolled down.

What's hairy and damp and sits shivering at fairs?
A coconut with a cold.

What's the difference between a square peg in a round
hole and a kilo of lard?
One's a fat lot of good and the other's a good lot of fat!

Baby Skunk: "But, Mom, why can't I have a chemistry
set for my birthday?"
Mother: "Because it would stink the house out, that's
why."

What happens when business is slow at a medicine factory?
You can hear a cough drop.

What do you get if you cross a witch with an ice cube?
A cold spell.

What is the most popular food served at a nudist camp?
Skinless sausages.

What's the best thing to put into a pizza?
Your teeth.

Which two letters are rotten for your teeth?
D K

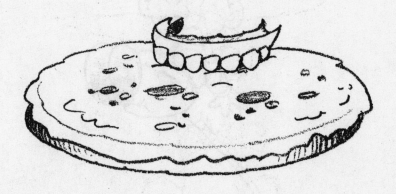

127

What did the "just married" spiders call their new home?
Newlywebs.

What did the monster say when he saw Snow White and the Seven Dwarfs?
"Yum, yum!"

"Why did you drop the baby?"
"Well, Mrs Smith said he was a bonny bouncing baby, so I wanted to see if he did."

The monster from outer space decided to go on a trip around the universe, so he went to the rocket office to book a ticket to the moon. "Sorry, sir," said the attendant, "the moon is full at the moment."

What did the werewolf write at the bottom of the letter?
Best vicious...

Did you hear about the lady ghoul who went to buy a dress in the Phantom Fashion boutique?
"I'd like to try on that shroud in the window," she told the ghoul in charge.
"Yes, Madam," said the ghoul, "but wouldn't you prefer to use the changing-room instead?"

The wonderful Wizard of Oz
Retired from business becoz
What with up to date science
To most of his clients
He wasn't the wiz that he woz.

"Waiter, waiter, there's a dead beetle in my gravy."
"Yes, sir. Beetles are terrible swimmers."

Anna: "I was top of the class last week."
Mom: "How did you manage that?"
Anna: "I managed to answer a question about elephants."
Mom: "What question?"
Anna: "Well, the teacher asked us how many legs an elephant had, and I said five."
Mom: "But that wasn't right."
Anna: "I know, but it was the nearest anyone got."

Keith: "Our teacher's an old bat."
Kevin: "You mean he's bad-tempered?"
Keith: "Not only that, he hangs around us all the time."

What happened when the werewolf met the five-headed monster?
It was love at first fright.

The Stock Market is a place where sheep and cattle are sold.

Kelly: "Is God a doctor, Miss?"
Teacher: "In some ways, Kelly. Why do you ask?"
Kelly: "Because the Bible says that the Lord gave the tablets to Moses."

What did the speak-your-weight machine say when the fat lady stepped on?
"One at a time, please."

"Did you hear about the idiot who invented the one piece jigsaw puzzle?"

Sign on the school noticeboard: Guitar for sale, cheap, no strings attached.

What happened to Ray when he met the man-eating monster?
He became an ex-Ray.

When Ben hit his thumb with a hammer he let out a few choice words. Shocked by her son's outburst, his mother said, "Don't you dare use that kind of language in here."
"William Shakespeare did," replied Ben.
"Well, you'd better stop going around with him," said mom.

Darren, at school dinner: "I've just swallowed a bone."
Teacher: "Are you choking?"
Darren: "No, I'm serious."

131

The cookery teacher was in a delicatessen buying nuts for the afternoon's cake baking. "What kind of nuts would you like?" asked the shop assistant.

"Cashew," replied the teacher.

"Bless you," said the shop assistant. "What kind of nuts would you like?"

In the summer holidays the math teacher collected information for a national opinion poll.

But after a week she was sacked. Her vital statistics were wrong.

What do you get when you cross an idiot with a watch?

A cuckoo clock.

First Teacher: "What's wrong with young Jimmy today? I saw him running round the playground screaming and pulling at his hair!"

Second Teacher: "Don't worry. He's just lost his marbles."

What does the music teacher do when he's locked out of the classroom?

Sing until he gets the right key.

How can you tell when it's rabbit pie for school dinner?
It has hares in it.

Girl: "Shall I put the kettle on?"
Boy: "No, I think you look alright in the dress you're wearing."

What do you get if you cross a caretaker with a monk who smokes large cigars?
A caretaker with a bad habit.

What kind of piano music do witches like best?
Hagtime.

Sign outside the school caretaker's hut: Will the person who took my ladder please return it, or further steps will be taken.

A monster walked into a shop selling dress fabrics and said, "I'd like 6 meters of pink satan for my wife."
"It's satin, sir, not satan," said assistant. "Satan is something that looks like the devil."
"Oh," said the monster, "you know my wife?"

Why was Harold called the space cadet when he was at school?
Because he had a lot of space between his ears.

Did you hear about the schoolboy who was so lazy he went around with his mouth open to save him the trouble of yawning?

Did you hear what Dumb Donald did when he offered to paint the garage for his Dad in the summer holidays?
The instructions said "put on three coats," so he went in and put on his blazer, his raincoat and his bomber jacket.

When George left school he was going to be a printer.
All the teachers said he was the right type.

134

Mary's class was taken to the Natural History Museum in London.

"Did you enjoy yourself?" asked her mother when she got home.

"Oh yes," replied Mary. "But it was funny going to a dead zoo."

Rob: "I must rush home and cut the lawn."

Teacher: "Did your father promise you something if you cut it?"

Rob: "No, he promised me something if I didn't!"

Miss Smith and Mrs Brown were having a chat over a cup of tea about why they entered the teaching profession. "I used to be a fortune teller before I became a teacher," said Miss Smith. "But I had to give it up, there wasn't any future in it."

Retired colonel, talking of the good old days: "Have you ever hunted bear?"

His grandson's teacher: "No, but I've been fishing in shorts."

Mrs Turbot, the biology teacher, was very fond of fish. She was also rather deaf, which was great for the children in her class. "What Mrs Turbot needs," said one of her colleagues, "is a herring-aid."

Two teachers were reminiscing about their deprived childhood. "I lived in a tough neighborhood," said the first. "People were afraid to walk the streets after dark." "That's nothing," said the other, "whenever I hung my Christmas stocking up by the fireplace, Santa Claus stole it."

It was a snowy day during the winter semester and Jimmy arrived very late. He started to list all the reasons for being late. First of all the alarm clock hadn't gone off. Then he'd had to help his father clear the snow from the drive. Then the bus had arrived late. Then the bus had got stuck trying to drive up the hill. Then.... The teacher cut him short. "It's all right, Jimmy," he said, "I get your drift."

School Doctor to Parent: "I'm afraid your daughter needs glasses."
Parent: "How can you tell?"
School Doctor: "By the way she came in through the window."

Games Master: "Why didn't you stop the ball?"
Hapless Harold: "I thought that was what the net was for."

Nigel: "You said the school dentist would be painless, but he wasn't."
Teacher: "Did he hurt you?"
Nigel: "No, but he screamed when I bit his finger."

What's the difference between an iced lolly and the school bully?
You lick one, the other licks you.

What's the difference between a gymnastics teacher and a duck?
One goes quick on its legs, the other goes quack on its legs.

Why was the cannibal expelled from school?
Because he kept buttering up the teacher.

Igor: "How was that science fiction movie you saw last night?
Dr Frankenstein: "Oh, the same old story – boy meets girl, boy loses girl, boy builds new girl..."

What do ghosts like in their coffee?
Evaporated milk.

What has two heads, three hands, two noses and five feet?
A monster with spare parts.

What should you call a polite, friendly, kind, good-looking monster?
A failure.

Dr Frankenstein: "How can I stop that monster charging?"
Igor: "Why not take away his credit card?"

NOT THERE!

Did you hear about the vain monster who was going bald?
The doctor couldn't do a hair transplant for him so he shrunk his head to fit his hair.

Teacher: "What do you know about Lake Erie?"
Rose: "It's full of ghosts, Miss."

"She's such a gossip she tells you what you were going to say to her before you have the chance to tell her."

Teacher: "And why would you like to be a teacher, Clarence?"
Clarence: "Because I wouldn't have to learn anything, Sir. I'd know everything by then."

What did the teacher say after spending thousands in the expensive hotel? "I'm sorry to leave, now that I've almost bought the place."

Teacher: "Name six things that contain milk."
Daft Dora: "Custard, cocoa, and four cows."

"I have two noses, three eyes and only one ear. What am I?"
"Very ugly."

"Waiter, do you serve crabs?"
"Sit down, Sir. We serve anybody."

Ronald had broken a rib playing rugby. He went to the doctor, who asked how he was feeling. "I keep getting a stitch in my side," he replied.
"That's good," said the doctor. "It shows the bone is knitting."

What is a man who tests people's eyes called?
An optimist.

140

Mrs Broadbeam: "Now, remember, children, travel is very good for you. It broadens the mind."
Sarah, muttering: "If you're anything to go by, that's not all it broadens!"

Brian: "Our school must have very clean kitchens."
Bill: "How can you tell?"
Brian: "All the food tastes of soap."

The math teacher and the English teacher went out for a quick pizza after school. "How long will the pizzas be?" asked the math teacher.
"Sorry, Sir," replied the waiter, "we don't do long pizzas, just ordinary round ones."

A teacher took her class for a walk in the country, and Susie found a grass snake. "Come quickly, Miss," she called, "here's a tail without a body!"

Why is a caretaker nothing like Robinson Crusoe?
Because Robinson Crusoe got all his work done by Friday.

Teacher to dinner lady: "A pork chop, please and make it lean."
Dinner Lady: "Certainly, Mr Smith, which way?"

Why did the music student have a piano in the bathroom?
Because he was practising Handel's Water Music.

Why did the old lady cover her mouth with her hands when she sneezed?
To catch her false teeth.

Why did the man go out and buy a set of tools?
Because everyone kept telling him he had a screw loose.

Wilberforce Witherspoon saw a notice outside a police station which read: MAN WANTED FOR ROBBERY.
So he went in and applied for the job!

"My Auntie Edna is so fat, Uncle Tom has to stand up in bed each morning to see if it's daylight."

Simple Simon was writing a geography essay. It began, "The people who live in Paris are called parasites...."

"My dad is stupid. He thinks a fjord is a Norwegian motor car."

Music Student: "Did you really learn to play the violin in six easy lessons?"
Music Teacher: "Yes, but the 500 that followed were pretty difficult."

Why is history like a fruit cake?
Because it's full of dates.

How do you catch a squirrel?
Climb up a tree and act like a nut.

Which animals do you have to beware of when you take exams?
Cheetahs.

Why did the champion monster give up boxing?
He didn't want to spoil his looks.

What's a ghost's favorite entertainment?
Going to the phantomime.

"Jimmy, how many more times must I tell you to come away from that biscuit barrel?"
"No more, mom. It's empty."

How did the Vikings communicate with one another?
By Norse code.

George knocked on the door of his friend's house.
When his friend's mother answered he said: "Can
Albert come out to play?"
"No," said the mother, "it's too cold."
"Well, then," said George, "can his football come out to
play?"

What was Noah's occupation?
Preserving pears.

There was a fight in the fish shop last night – a whole
lot of fish got battered!

1st Witch: "I like your toad. He always has such a nice
expression on his face."
2nd Witch: "It's because he's a hoptimist."

Why did the elephant paint her head yellow?
To see if blondes really do have more fun.

"Doctor, doctor, I keep seeing double."
"Take a seat, please."
"Which one?"

Which vegetable goes best with jacket potatoes?
Button mushrooms.

Woman in bed: "Aaagh! Aaagh! A ghost just floated
into my room!"
Ghost: "Don't worry, madam, I'm just passing through."

Two shipwrecked sailors managed to climb onto an
iceberg. "Oh, dear," said the first, "do you think we'll
survive?"
"Of course we will," said the second. "Look, here
comes the *Titanic*."

What airline do vampires travel on?
British Scareways.

Mr and Mrs Blenkinsop were always fighting. Then one morning as Mrs Blenkinsop was going to the laundrette she was knocked down by a hit and run driver. A policeman rushed up and asked her if she'd taken the car's number. "I didn't need to," replied Mrs Blenkinsop. "It was my husband in that car."
"Did you see him?" asked the policeman.
"No," said Mrs Blenkinsop, "but I'd know that laugh anywhere."

What happened when the idiot had a brain transplant?
The brain rejected him.

What's the difference between a nail and a boxer?
One gets knocked in, the other gets knocked out.

A man arrived at a seaside hotel where he had made a reservation rather late at night. All the lights were out, so he knocked on the door. After a long time a light appeared in an upstairs window and a woman called out, "Who are you? What do you want?"

"I'm John Jackson," he called. "I'm staying here."

"Stay there, then," she retorted, and slammed the window shut!

Two fleas were sitting on Robinson Crusoe's back as he lay on the beach in the sun. "Well, so long," said one to the other, "I'll see you on Friday."

"Dad, that Mr Jenkins down the road said you weren't fit to live with pigs!"

"What did you say, son?"

"I stuck up for you. I said you were certainly fit to live with pigs."

A pilot flying over the jungle was having trouble with his plane and decided to bail out before it crashed. So he got into his parachute, jumped, pulled the rip-cord, and drifted gently down to land. Unfortunately he landed right in a large cooking pot which a tribal chief was simmering gently over a fire. The chief looked at him, rubbed his eyes, looked again, and asked, "What's this flier doing in my soup?"

"Mum, are the Higginbottoms very poor people?"
"I don't think so, Jimmy. Why do you ask?"
"Because they made such a fuss when their baby
swallowed a 50 cent coin."

Two fishermen were out in their boat one day when a
hand appeared in the ocean.
"What's that?" asked the first fisherman. "It looks as if
someone's drowning!"
"Nonsense," said the second. "It was just a little wave."

Did you hear about the stupid photographer?
He saved burned-out lightbulbs for use in his
darkroom.

"I can't get over that new beard of yours. It makes your
face look just like a busted sofa."

What kind of bandage do people wear after heart
surgery?
Ticker tape.

Did you hear about Mrs Dimwit's new baby? She thought babies should be pink, so she took this one to the doctor because it was a horrible yeller.

What's black and white, black and white, black and white?
A nun rolling down a hill.

Did you hear about the woman who was so keen on road safety that she always wore white at night? Last winter she was knocked down by a snow plow.

What did one magician say to another?
"Who was that girl I sawed you with last night?"

What did one cannibal say to another?
"Who was that girl I saw you with last night?"
"That was no girl, that was my supper."

Did you hear about the village idiot buying bird seed?
He said he wanted to grow some birds.

Did you hear about the boy who got worried when his
nose grew to eleven inches long?
He thought it might turn into a foot.

What kind of jokes does a chiropodist like?
Corny jokes.

How many skunks does it take to make a big stink?
A phew!

What do you do if you split your sides laughing?
Run until you get a stitch.

"Doctor, doctor, I think I've been bitten by a vampire."
"Drink this glass of water."
"Will it make me better?"
"No, but I'll be able to see if your neck leaks."

First cannibal woman: "I just don't know what to make
of my husband these days."
Second cannibal woman: "How about a curry?"

What was the fly doing in the alphabet soup?
Learning to spell.

How can you tell an old person from a young person?
An old person can sing and brush their teeth at the
same time.

152

Mr Smooth was ordering a meal in a restaurant and was horrified to see that the waiter was covered with pimples.
"Have you got acne?" he asked.
"No," replied the waiter, "just what you can see on the menu."

What did one skeleton say to the other?
"If we had any guts we'd get out of here."

Whom does a monster ask for a date?
Any old ghoul he can find.

What did Enormous Eric win when he lost 50 pounds in weight?
The No-Belly Prize.

Why was the man arrested for looking at sets of dentures in a dentist's window?
Because it was against the law to pick your teeth in public.

What do you do if your nose goes on strike?
Picket.

Do undertakers enjoy their job?
Of corpse they do.

"Mommy, Mommy, I don't like Daddy!"
"Well, just eat the salad then, dear."

"My girlfriend thinks I'm a great wit."
"Well, she's nearly right."

Teacher: "Didn't you know the bell had gone?"
Silly Sue: "I didn't take it, Miss."

Teacher: "Peter! Why are you scratching yourself?"
Peter: " 'Cos no one else knows where I itch."

Where do ghouls go to study?
Ghoullege.

Ghoul: "Your little ghoul's grown!"
Mrs Ghoul: "Yes, she's certainly gruesome."

Teacher, in pet shop: "I'd like to buy a budgie, please.
How much do they cost?"
Pet shop owner: "$10 apiece."
Teacher, horrified: "How much does a whole one
cost?"

Teacher: Fred! Wipe that mud off your shoes before
you come in the classroom."
Fred: "But, Sir, I'm not wearing any shoes."

Knock, knock.
Who's there?
Sacha.
Sacha who?
Sacha lot of questions in this exam!

There were ten zebras in the zoo. All but nine
escaped. How many were left?
Nine!

Teacher: "Who can tell me what an archaeologist is?"
Tracey: "It's someone whose career is in ruins."

What do you get if you cross a caretaker with an
elephant?
A 20-ton school cleaner.

What's the difference between a caretaker and a bad-
tempered teacher?
Is there any difference?

Teacher: "Why are you late, Penelope?"
Penelope: "I was obeying the sign that says 'Children –
Dead Slow,' Miss."

Teacher: "Barbara, name three collective nouns."
Barbara: "The wastepaper bin, the garbage bin and the
vacuum cleaner."

Hil: "Who was the fastest runner in history?"
Bill: "Adam. He was first in the human race."

Teacher: "I'd like a room, please."
Hotel Receptionist: "Single, Sir?"
Teacher: "Yes, but I am engaged."

Did you hear about the teacher who was trying to instil
good table manners in her girls? She told them, "A
well-brought-up girl never crumbles her bread or rolls
in her soup."

What do ghosts do at 11 am?
Take a coffin break.

Monica fancied herself as an artist. But her teacher
said she was so bad it was a wonder she could draw
breath.

Teacher: "Who knows what a hippy is?"
Clever Dick: "It's something that holds your leggy on."

Parent to School Doctor: "Will those pills really cure
my little Amy?"
School Doctor: "Well, no one I've given them to has
ever come back."

Why are pianos so noble?
Because they're either upright or grand.

Why did Silly Sue throw her guitar away?
Because it had a hole in the middle.

Henry: "I'd like to learn to play a drum, Sir."
Music Teacher: "Beat it!"

Did you hear about Miss Spellbinder's new twins?
It's difficult to tell witch from witch.

Why are vampires artistic?
They're good at drawing blood.

A horrible old witch surprised all her friends by
announcing that she was going to get married. "But,"
said another old hag, "you always said men were
stupid. And you vowed never to marry."
"Yes, I know," said the witch. "But I finally found one
who asked me."

What did the mother ghost say to the naughty baby
ghost?
Spook when you're spooken to.

Dr Frankenstein: "I've just invented something that
everyone in the world will want! You know how you get
a nasty ring around the bathtub every time you use it,
and you have to clean the ring off?"
Igor: "Yes, I hate it."
Dr Frankenstein: "Well you need never have a bathtub
ring again! I've invented the square tub...."

1st Witch: "Every time it's misty, I hear a strange
croaking noise coming from your house."
2nd Witch: "That would be my frog horn."

The four-legged monster's wife went to the doctor's surgery. "One of my husband's legs has just fallen off," she wailed. "Could you supply a wooden one for him?" The doctor agreed and gave her a wooden leg and off she went. A few days later she was back. "You'll never believe it, doctor, but another of his legs has fallen off. Do you have another spare?"

The doctor looked in his cupboard, found one and gave it to her, thinking that this was a bit odd. He thought it was even more odd when she returned the following week to say that a third of her husband's legs had fallen off, but he dutifully supplied another replacement. But when she came back only a couple of days later he decided that enough was enough.

"I think I should see your husband," he said. "To lose all four legs is a real disaster. He may be seriously ill." The lady monster looked at him for a minute, then burst into tears. "It's no good, I can't keep lying to you," she sobbed. "The truth is, my husband's making a coffee table...."

Did you hear about the boy who was told to do 100 lines? He drew 100 cats on the paper. He thought the teacher had said "lions."

What kind of monster has the best hearing?
The eeriest.

How can you tell if you've had a monster in your fridge?
It leaves footprints in the butter.

What happened when the Ice Monster ate a curry?
He blew his cool.

What happened when the headmistress's poodle swallowed a role of film?
Nothing serious developed.

Mother: "Did you enjoy the school outing, dear?"
Jane: "Yes. And we're going again tomorrow."
Mother: "Really? Why's that?"
Jane: "To try and find the kids we left behind."

What has eight feet and sings?
The school quartet.

"What's your handicrafts teacher like?"
"She's a sew and sew."

Teacher: "What's a robin?"
John: "A bird that steals, Miss."

Which ghost sailed the seven seas looking for rubbish
and blubber?
The ghost of BinBag the Whaler.

After years of traveling around the world in his search, the wicked Abanazar finally discovered the enchanted cave in which he believed lay the magic lamp which would make him millions. He stood before the boulders which sealed the cave, and uttered the magic words, "Open sesame!"
There was a silence, and then a ghastly voice from within moaned, "Open says-a-who?"

Did you hear about the lady monster who was so determined to be beautiful that she put on vanishing cream, anti-wrinkle cream, moisturizing lotion, and vitamin E cream? It didn't work, though. In fact it turned her black and blue, because every night she kept sliding out of bed.

What did the cannibal say when he met the famous explorer?
"Dr Livingstone, I consume?"

Why did the cyclops apply for half a television license?
Because he only had one eye.

What is black and has eight wheels?
A witch on roller skates.

1st Witch: "My dustbin must be full of toadstools."
2nd Witch: "Why's that?"
1st Witch: "There's not mushroom inside."

Witch: "Try some of my sponge cake."
Wizard: "It's a bit tough."
Witch: "That's strange. I only bought the sponge from the chemist this morning."

Superman climbed to the top of a high mountain in the middle of the African jungle. As he reached the summit he found himself suddenly surrounded by dozens of vicious vampires, ghosts, monsters and goblins. What did he say?
"Boy, am I in the wrong joke!"

Spook: "Should you eat spiders and slugs and zombie slime on an empty stomach?"
Witch: "No, you should eat them on a plate."

A man out for a walk came across a little boy pulling his cat's tail. "Hey, you!" he called. "Don't pull the cat's tail!"
"I'm not pulling!" replied the little boy. "I'm only holding on – the cat's doing the pulling!"

How did the invisible boy upset his mother?
He kept appearing.

What happened when Dr Frankenstein swallowed
some uranium?
He got atomic ache.

Did you hear about the stupid monster who hurt
himself while he was raking up leaves?
He fell out of a tree.

Two ghouls were in the middle of an argument. "I didn't
come here to be insulted," yelled one.
"Really? Where do you usually go?"

What gets bigger the more you take away?
A hole.

Did you hear about the snooker-mad monster? He went to the doctor because he didn't feel well. "What do you eat?" asked the doctor.
"For breakfast I have a couple of red snooker balls, and at lunchtime I grab a black, a pink and two yellows. I have a brown with my tea in the afternoon, and then a blue and another pink for dinner."
"I know why you're not feeling well," exclaimed the doctor. "You're not getting enough greens."

Dracula: "Have you seen the new monster from Poland?"
Frankenstein: "A Pole?"
Dracula: "Yes – you can tell from his wooden expression."

Did you hear about the monster with one eye at the back of his head, and one at the front? He was terribly moody because he couldn't see eye to eye with himself.

Rumors that Count Dracula is about to marry Glenda the Ghoul are not true. They're just good fiends, that's all.

Dr Frankenstein decided to build an extension to his laboratory, so he crossed a cement mixer, a ghoul and a chicken. Now he's got a demon bricklayer.

What did the angry monster do when he got his gas
bill?
He exploded.

Why did the wooden monsters stand in a circle?
They were having a board meeting.

Frankenstein: "Help, I've got a short circuit!"
Igor: "Don't worry, I'll lengthen it."

1st Monster: "Where do fleas go in winter?"
Werewolf: "Search me!"

What comes out at night and goes "Munch, munch,
ouch!"
A vampire with a rotten tooth.

Witch: "I've never been so insulted in my life! I went to a Halloween party, and at midnight they asked me to take my mask off."
Spook: "Why are you so angry?"
Witch: "I wasn't wearing a mask."

What did the shy pebble monster say?
"I wish I was a little boulder."

Why did the undertaker chop all his corpses into little bits?
Because he liked them to rest in pieces.

1st Monster: "Every time we meet, you remind me of a famous film star."
2nd Monster: "Meryl Streep? Madonna? Raquel Welch?"
1st Monster: "No, ET"

How do monsters count to 13?
On their fingers.

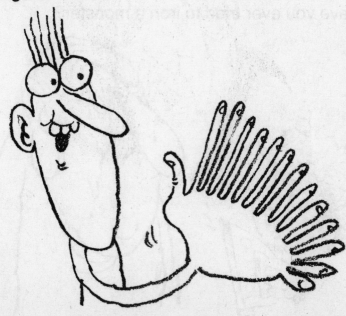

How do they count to 47?
They take off their socks and count their toes.

Boris the monster knocked on a witch's door and asked for something to eat. "You look familiar," said the witch. "Didn't I give you some bat's blood soup last week?" "Yes," said the monster, "but I'm better now."

The vampire went into the Monster Cafe. "Shark and chips," he ordered. "And make it snappy."

Father monster came home from the Monster Repair Company to find his son Boris in disgrace. "He's been fighting again," said his wife, "it's those terrible Slime children down the road. They're such a bad influence on him. He learned all about punching and kicking from them."
"Yes," interrupted Boris, "but hitting them on the head with an axe was my idea."

Why are most monsters covered in wrinkles?
Have you ever tried to iron a monster?

Monster: "I'm so ugly."
Ghost: "It's not that bad!"
Monster: "It is! When my grandfather was born they passed out cigars. When my father was born they just passed out cigarettes. When I was born they simply passed out."

What is even more invisible than the invisible ghost?
His shadow.

Ghost: "I've been invited to an avoidance."
Monster: "An avoidance? What's that?"
Ghost: "It's a dance for people who hate each other."

Why do monsters wear glasses?
So that they don't bump into other monsters.

Igor: "Dr Frankenstein's just invented a new kind of glue."
Dracula: "I hope it doesn't make him stuck up."

Why did the monster take a dead man for a drive in his car?
Because he was a car-case.

What should you do if a zombie borrows your comic?
Wait for him to give it back.

Sarah: "Did you hear about Samantha now she's left school? She's working for a company that makes blotting paper."
Selina: "Does she enjoy it?"
Sarah: "I believe she finds it very absorbing."

Spooky happenings at the supermarket! A customer was just leaning over the freezer looking for some frozen chips when ten fish fingers crept up and pulled him in....

Why do demons get on so well with ghouls?
Because demons are a ghoul's best friend.

How did dinosaurs pass exams?
With extinction.

Did you hear the story of the three holes?
Well, well, well.

Simon: "My girlfriend and I fell out last night. She
wanted to go and watch ice-skating, but I wanted to go
to the football match."
Peter: "What was the ice-skating like?"

What's a skeleton?
Bones with the person off.

What is a skeleton? Someone who went on a diet and
forgot to say "when."

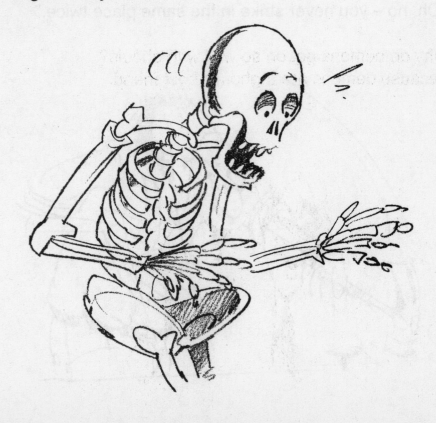

Why was the insect thrown out of the forest?
Because he was a litter bug.

My auntie has a sore throat. What should she do?
Take auntie-septic.

What did the undertaker say to his girlfriend?
"Em-balmy about you."

What happened when the pussy swallowed a penny?
There was money in the kitty.

A young lad was helping his dad with do-it-yourself
jobs around the house. "You know, son," said the
father, "you're just like lightning with that hammer."
"Fast, eh?" said the boy.
"Oh, no – you never strike in the same place twice."

Pattie: "We had a burglary last night, and they took everything except the soap and towels."
Peter: "The dirty crooks."

Who's stronger than a muscleman who can tear up a telephone directory?
Someone who can tear up a street.

Why are Martians green?
Because they forgot to take their travel-sickness tablets.

What does Dracula say to his victims?
"It's been nice gnawing you."

What did the traffic light say to the motorist?
"Don't look now, I'm changing."

What do ghosts wear if they're short-sighted?
Spooktacles.

"Doctor, doctor, I don't like all these flies buzzing around my head."
"Pick out the ones you like and I'll swat the rest."

Who carries a sack and bites people?
Santa Jaws.

Arthur: "It's true that there is a connection between television and violence."
Martha: "What makes you think that?"
Arthur: "Because I told my teacher I had watched television instead of doing my homework, and she hit me."

"I can't understand why people say my girlfriend's legs look like matchsticks. They do look like sticks – but they certainly don't match."

176

"What's your dad getting for Christmas?"
"Bald and fat."

Ben's new girlfriend uses such greasy lipstick that he has to sprinkle his face with sand to get a better grip.

Albert Littleun is so small his chin has a rash from his bootlaces.

What did the neurotic pig say to the farmer?
"You take me for grunted."

"Doctor, doctor, I keep thinking I'm a pair of curtains!"
"Pull yourself together, man."

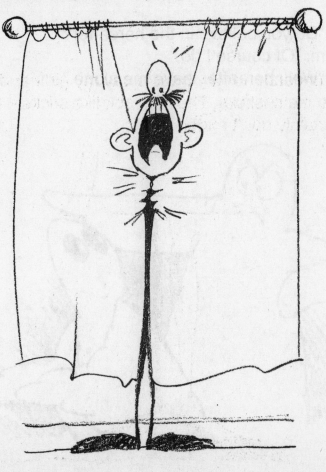

"She's the kind of girl that boys look at twice – they can't believe it the first time."

"Every time I take my girlfriend out for a meal she eats her head off."
"She looks better that way."

"What's the difference between a Peeping Tom and someone who's just got out of the bath?
"One is rude and nosey. The other is nude and rosy."

"Some girls who are the picture of health are just painted that way."

Ghost: "Do you believe in the hereafter?"
Phantom: "Of course I do."
Ghost: "Well, hereafter leave me alone."

Why did Dracula eat strong peppermints?
Because he had bat breath.

Waiter: "And how did you find your meat, sir?"
Customer: "Oh, I just lifted a potato and there it was."

Why did the lazy idiot apply for a job in a bakery?
He fancied a long loaf.

"You are so ugly your face would stop a clock."
"And yours would make one run."

Patient: "Tell me honestly, how am I?"
Dentist: "Your teeth are fine, but your gums will have to come out."

"Mum's cooking is improving. The smoke is not as black as it used to be!"

"Yes, I do like your dress – but isn't it a little early for halloween?"

"You must think I'm a perfect idiot."
"No, you're not perfect."

"What's the difference between a sigh, a car and a monkey?"
"A sigh is oh dear. A car is too dear. A monkey is you, dear."

Soprano at concert: "And what would you like me to sing next?"
Member of audience: "Do you know 'Old Man River'?"
Soprano: "Er, yes."
Member of audience: "Well go jump in it."

What did the beaver say to the tree?
It sure is good to gnaw you.

Cannibal in restaurant: "I don't think much of your chef."
Waiter: "In that case, just eat the salad."

Why was the ghost arrested?
He didn't have a haunting licence.

Why are fried onions like a photocopying machine?
They keep repeating themselves.

Was the carpenter's son a chip off the old block?

Why is it bad to upset a cannibal?
You end up in hot water.

Did you hear about the little spook who couldn't sleep at night because his brother kept telling him human stories?

What did they say about the aristocratic monster?
That he was born with a silver shovel in his mouth.

Harry: "Please may I have another pear, Miss?"
Teacher: "Another, Harry? They don't grow on trees, you know."

What happens if you tell a psychiatrist you are schizophrenic?
He charges you double.

Why did the lady monster wear curlers at night?
She wanted to wake up curly in the morning.

"Do you serve women in this bar?"
"No sir, you have to bring your own."

"I don't care who you are, get those reindeer off my roof."

"I don't know what it is that makes you stupid but whatever it is, it works."

A flute player was walking home late one night from a concert. He took a short cut through the local woods, and he hadn't gone far before he bumped into a ghost and then a vampire. Pulling out his flute he began to play a lovely trilling melody – the ghost and the vampire stood entranced. Soon the musician was surrounded by a crowd of phantoms, monsters, goblins, cannibals and witches listening to the music. Then up bounded a werewolf. "Yum! Yum!" he growled, and he gobbled up the flute player.
"Why did you do that?" complained the others. "We were enjoying it."
"Eh, what was that?" said the werewolf.

Why was the sword-swallowing monster put in prison?
He coughed and killed two people.

A man who forgets his wife's birthday is certain to get
something to remember her by.

Teacher: "Can anyone tell me what a shamrock is?"
Jimmy: "It's a fake diamond, Miss."

"My dad is so short-sighted he can't get to sleep
unless he counts elephants."

"Doctor, doctor, can you give me something for my
baldness?"
"How about a few pounds of pig manure?"
"Will that cure my baldness?"
"No, but with that on your head no one will come near
enough to notice that you're bald."

Two people went into a very dark, spooky cave. "I can't see a thing," said one.
"Hold my hand," said the other.
"All right." The first man reached out. "Take off that horrible bristly glove first, though."
"But I'm not wearing a glove..."

Why don't centipedes play football?
Because by the time they've got their boots on it's time to go home.

What happens if you play table-tennis with a bad egg?
First it goes ping, then it goes pong.

What's the difference between a coyote and a flea?
One howls on the prairie, and the other prowls on the hairy.

Donald: "My canary died of flu."
Dora: "I didn't know canaries got flu."
Donald: "Mine flew into a car."

"Doctor, doctor, I've got a little stye."
"Then you'd better buy a little pig."

What did the zombie say when he knocked on Eddie's door?
"Eddie body home?"

Did you hear about the man who ate 106 cloves of garlic a day? He was taken to hospital in a coma. Doctors said it was from inhaling his own breath.

Who is Wyatt Burp?
The sheriff with the repeater.

Golfer: "Caddy, why do you keep looking at your watch?"
Caddy: "It's not a watch, it's a compass."

Did you hear about the Irish boy who had a soft spot for his math teacher?
It was a bog in the middle of Ireland.

Did you hear about the stupid angler who poured whisky into the river? He thought the fish would come up ready canned.

How do fleas travel from place to place?
By itch hiking.

Teacher: "Are you really going to leave school, Ben, or are you just saying that to brighten my day?"

Did you hear about the time Eddy's sister tried to make a birthday cake?
The candles melted in the oven.

"My dad is rather tired this morning. Last night he dreamed he was working."

"Doctor, doctor, I'm nervous, this is the first brain operation I've had."
"Don't worry, it's the first I've performed."

Did you hear about the horrible hairy monster who did farmyard impressions?
He didn't do the noises, he just made the smells.

Why are school cooks cruel?
Because they batter fish and beat eggs.

In the good old days, husbands used to come home from work, and say: "What's cooking?"
Now they say: "What's thawing?"

188

Knock, knock.
Who's there?
Bella.
Bella who?
Bella not working, that's why I knocka.

Why did the stupid pilot land his plane on a house?
Because the landing lights were on.

"How do you make someone burn his ear?"
"Ring him up when he is ironing."

If you watch the way that many motorists drive you will
soon reach the conclusion that the most dangerous
part of a car is the nut behind the wheel.

First Woman: "Whenever I'm down in the dumps I buy
myself a new hat."
Second Woman: "Oh, so that's where you get them."

Wife: "Shall I give that tramp one of my cakes?"
Husband: "Why, what harm has he ever done us?"

"My uncle spent a fortune on deodorants before he found out that people didn't like him anyway."

"It was so hot when we went on holiday last year that we had to take turns sitting in each other's shadow."

What is small, pink, wrinkly, and belongs to Grandpa?
Grandma.

"I can't understand the critics saying that only an idiot would like that television program. I really enjoyed it."

Why was the headmaster not pleased when he bumped into an old friend?
They were both driving their cars at the time.

What's the difference between a schoolteacher and a train?
A schoolteacher says, "Spit out that toffee" and a train says, "Choo, choo."

Did you hear about the ogre who threw trunks over cliffs? Nothing special about that, you might think – but the elephants were still attached.

What's the best way of stopping a monster sliding through the eye of a needle?
Tie a knot in his neck.

Why did the monster drink ten liters of anti-freeze?
So that he didn't have to buy a winter coat.

How do you know when there's a monster hiding under your bed?
When you wake up, your nose is squashed up against the ceiling.

Why does Dracula always travel with his coffin?
Because his life is at stake.

Why don't you go home and brush up on your ignorance?

What's a giant's favorite tale?
A tall story.

What did the monster say when he saw Santa Claus?
"Yum, yum."

Anne: "Ugh! The water in my glass is cloudy."
Dan, trying to impress his new girlfriend: "It's all right, it's just the glass that hasn't been washed."

Did you hear about the witch who fed her pet vulture on sawdust? The vulture laid ten eggs and when they hatched, nine chicks had wooden legs and the tenth was a woodpecker.

"How does your head feel today?"
"As good as new."
"It should be as good as new – it's never been used."

Why did the teacher call both her children Ed?
Because she thought two Eds were better than one.

Knock, knock.
Who's there?
Gopher.
Gopher who?
Gopher a walk over the cliff.

Why did the school orchestra have bad manners?
Because it didn't know how to conduct itself.

Robot: "I have to dry my feet carefully after a bath."
Monster: "Why?"
Robot: "Otherwise I get rusty nails."

Why is it difficult to open a piano?
Because all the keys are inside.

Caspar: "I was the teacher's pet last year."
Jaspar: "Why was that?"
Caspar: "She couldn't afford a dog."

Why was the student witch so bad at essays?
Because she couldn't spell properly.

"My sister thinks that a juggernaut is an empty beer mug."

Did you hear about the boy who had to do a project on trains?
He had to keep track of everything!

Where do witches' frogs sit?
On toadstools.

How do you stop a werewolf howling in the back of a car?
Put him in the front.

What did the Eskimo children sing when their headmaster was leaving?
Freeze a Jolly Good Fellow.

My uncle is the meanest man in the world. He recently found a crutch – then he broke his leg so he could use it.

Bacon discovered the magnifying glass. At our local cafe you need a magnifying glass to discover the bacon.

Teacher: "Who can tell me where Turkey is?"
Dumb Donald: "We ate ours last Christmas, Miss."

How can a teacher increase the size of her pay check? By looking at it through a magnifying glass.

Ben's teacher regards Ben as a wonder child. He wonders whether he'll ever learn anything.

"Daddy, daddy, can I have another glass of water please?"
"But that's the tenth one I've given you tonight."
"Yes, but the baby's bedroom is still on fire."

"I've got a good idea."
"Must be beginners luck."

What kind of ghosts haunt hospitals?
Surgical spirits.

What's the difference between a vampire and a biscuit?
You can't dip a vampire in your tea.

There was a fierce chief of the Sioux
Who into a gun barrel blioux
To see if it was loaded;
The rifle exploded
As he should have known it would dioux!

197

Knock, knock.
Who's there?
Alison.
Alison who?
Alison to my teacher!

Geography teacher: "What is the coldest place in the world?"
Ann: "Chile."

Knock, knock.
Who's there?
Quiet Tina.
Quiet Tina who?
Quiet Tina classroom.

The first commandment was when Eve told Adam to eat the apple.

Today, every Tom, Dick and Harry is called Wayne.

Dim Dinah wrote in her exercise book: Margarine is butter made from imitation cows.

Which day of the week do ghosts like best?
Moandays.

How do hens dance?
Chick to chick.

The class went to a concert. Afterwards Jacqui asked the music teacher why members of the orchestra kept looking at a book while they played.
"Those books are the score," replied the teacher.
"Really?" replied Jacqui, "who was winning?"

Trees are planted to stop the wind. A larch can break wind at 40 meters.

Monster: "Someone told me Dr Frankenstein invented the safety match."
Igor: "Yes, that was one of his most striking achievements."

"I reckon Mom must be at least 30 years old – I counted the rings under her eyes."

What did the dragon say when he saw St George in his shining armor?
Oh no, not more tinned food.

The kidneys are infernal organs.

A catcall is when someone goes out at night saying, "Puss, puss, puss."

An allegory is when something disagrees with you and brings you out in a rash.

What's the definition of a good actor?
Somebody who tries hard to be everybody but himself.

Why did the composer spend all his time in bed?
He wrote sheet music.

What should a teacher take if he's run down?
The number of the car that hit him.

Teacher: "Why are you always late?"
Roger: "I threw away my alarm clock."
Teacher: "But why did you throw away your alarm clock?"
Roger: "Because it always went off when I was asleep."

Why did the child take a sledgehammer to school?
It was the day they broke up.

Teacher: "Why did the Romans build straight roads?"
Alex: "So the Britons couldn't lie in ambush round the corners."

What is brown, hairy, wears dark glasses and carries a pile of exercise books?
A coconut disguised as a teacher.

Why did the teacher put corn in his shoes?
Because he had pigeon toes.

What do you call a deaf teacher?
Anything you like, he can't hear you.

Music Teacher: "Do you like opera, Francesca?"
Francesca: "Apart from the singing, yes."

When is the water in the shower room musical?
When it's piping hot.

What takes a lot of licks from a teacher without
complaint?
An ice-cream.

What makes an ideal present for a monster?
Five pairs of gloves – one for each hand.

Did you hear that Dumb Donald got splinters in his fingers?
He'd been scratching his head!

How can a teacher double his money?
By folding it in half.

School Doctor: "Have you ever had trouble with appendicitis?"
Naomi: "Only when I tried to spell it."

How do teachers dress in mid-January?
Quickly.

What do you get if you cross a burglar with a concrete mixer?
A hardened criminal.

Why did the mean teacher walk around with her purse open?
She'd read there was going to be some change in the weather.

Did you hear about the spook who went on a high fiber diet?
He had beans on ghost twice a day.

"Doctor, doctor, it's wonderful! I feel like my old self again."
"In that case we'd better start a new course of treatment."

Which hand should you use to stir your tea?
Neither – you should use a spoon!

Barbara: "I wish I'd been alive a few hundred years ago."
History teacher: "Why?"
Barbara: "There'd have been a lot less history to learn."

Teacher: "Write 'I must not forget my gym kit' 100 times."
Nicky: "But, Sir, I only forgot it once."

What kind of musical instrument can you use for fishing?
The cast-a-net.

Science teacher: "What happened when electricity was first discovered?"
Alex: "Someone got a nasty shock."

Do men always snore?
No. Only when they're asleep.

Teacher: "What is meant by doggerel?"
Terry: "Little dogs, Miss."

English Teacher: "Now give me a sentence using the word 'fascinate.' "
Clara: "My raincoat has ten buttons but I can only fasten eight."

Why was Cinderella thrown out of the school's netball team?
Because she kept running away from the ball.

Mary arrived home from school covered in spots.
"Whatever's the matter?" asked her mother.
"I don't know," replied Mary, "but the teacher thinks I may have caught decimals."

How can you save school dumplings from drowning?
Put them in gravy boats.

Knock, knock.
Who's there?
Noah.
Noah who?
Noah good place to eat?

What's the best way of avoiding infection from biting ghosts?
Don't bite any ghosts.

1st Witch: "I'm not ugly. I could marry anyone I pleased!"
2nd Witch: "But that's the problem – you don't please anyone."

Why did Rupert eat six school dinners?
He wanted to be a big success.

"Was the headmaster's brother really a missionary?"
"He certainly was. He gave the people of the Cannibal Islands their first taste of Christianity."

What did the Eskimo schoolboy say to the Eskimo schoolgirl?
"What's an ice girl like you doing in a place like this?"

What can a schoolboy keep and give away at the same time?
A cold.

What's the difference between a crossword expert, a greedy boy and a pot of glue?
A crossword expert is a good puzzler and the greedy boy's a pud guzzler. The pot of glue? Ah, that's where you get stuck.

Why did the teacher wear a lifejacket at night?
Because she liked sleeping on a water bed, and couldn't swim!

Why is a pupil learning to sing like someone opening a tin of sardines?
Because they both have trouble with the key.

Why did the ghost's trousers fall down?
Because he had no visible means of support.

What's the very lowest game you can play?
Baseball.

Teacher: "Why do birds fly south in winter?"
Jim: "Because it's too far to walk."

Teacher: "Can you say your name backwards, Simon?"
Simon: "No, Mis."

Teacher: "Who can tell me what 'dogma' means?"
Cheeky Charlie: "It's a lady dog that's had puppies, Sir."

Countess Dracula: "Say something soft and sweet to me."
Dracula: "Marshmallows, chocolate fudge cake..."

What game do little cannibals like to play at parties?
Swallow my leader.

And what game do little ghosts play at parties?
Haunt the thimble.

A little monster was learning to play the violin. "I'm good, aren't I?" he asked his big brother.
"You should be on the radio," said the brother.
"You think I'm that good?"
"No, I think you're terrible, but at least if you were on the radio, I could switch you off."

What's a cannibal's favorite drink?
Wine with a lot of body.

Knock, knock.
Who's there?
Ida.
Ida who?
Ida nawful time at school today.

Knock, knock.
Who's there?
Genoa.
Genoa who?
Genoa good teacher?

How did the teacher knit a suit of armor?
She used steel wool.

Ghost: "I've decided to hang up my shroud and join the land of the living."
Ghoul: "You haven't?!?"
Ghost: "No, not really – April Ghoul!"

Geography teacher: "How can you prove that the world is round?"
Ben: "But I never said it was, Sir."

"I'm speechless."
"Good, just stay that way."

"Doctor, doctor, I keep thinking I'm a canary."
"I can't tweet you, go and see a vet."

"My girlfriend is a beautiful redhead – no hair, just a red head."

"Doctor, doctor, I can't stand being three feet tall any longer."
"Then you'll just have to learn to be a little patient."

If you have a referee in football, and an umpire in cricket, what do you have in bowls?
Goldfish.

"Doctor, doctor, I've only got 50 seconds to live."
"Just sit over there a minute."

What's Dracula's favorite society?
The Consumer's Association.

Did you hear about the Irish monster who went to night school to learn to read in the dark?

Father: "Would you like a pocket calculator for Christmas, son?"
Danny: "No thanks, Dad. I know how many pockets I've got."

1st Monster: "That orange and red checked coat of yours is a bit loud."
2nd Monster: "It's okay when I put my muffler on."

Clarrie: "Our math teacher has long black hair all down her back."
Barry: "Yes, it's a pity it doesn't grow on her head."

What do you get if you try to take a ghost's photograph?
Transparencies.

Did you hear about Dr Frankenstein's invention for cooking breakfast? He crossed a chicken with an electric organ and now he's got Hammond eggs.

What's the difference between a kangaroo, a lumberjack and a bag of peanuts?
A kangaroo hops and chews and a lumberjack chops and hews."
"Yes, but what's the bag of peanuts for?"
"For monkeys like you."

Who speaks at the ghosts' press conference?
The spooksperson.

What is Count Dracula's favorite snack?
A fangfurter.

Why is a complaining teacher the easiest to satisfy?
Because nothing satisfies them.

Woman: "If you were my husband I'd poison your coffee."
Man: "And if you were my wife, I'd drink it."

Why did the monster walk over the hill?
It was too much bother to walk under it.

What's the cannibal's favorite restaurant called?
Man Alive.

What do you get if you cross your least favorite teacher with a telescope?
A horrorscope.

"Joan, pick up your feet when you walk."
"What for, Mom? I've only got to put them down again."

What do ghosts eat for breakfast?
Dreaded wheat.

What did one ghost say to another?
"I'm sorry, but I just don't believe in people."

How do ghosts keep their feet dry?
By wearing boo-ts.

1st Ghost: "I saw *The Phantom of the Opera* last night, on television."
2nd Ghost: "Was it frightening?"
1st Ghost: "Yes, it half scared the life into me!"

What is a ghost's favorite dessert?
Boo-berry pie with I-scream.

Why are ghosts invisible?
They wear see-through clothes.

What do ghostly soldiers say to strangers?
"Who ghost there?"

Why is the graveyard such a noisy place?
Because of all the coffin!

What do you do with a green ghost?
Wait until he is ripe.

1st Ghost: "I find haunting castles really boring these days."
2nd Ghost: "I know what you mean. I just don't seem to be able to put any life into it."

Which is the ghost's favorite stretch of water?
Lake Eerie.

What do ghosts like about riding horses?
Ghoulloping.

What do you get if you cross a ghost with a packet of crisps?
Snacks that go crunch in the night.

What did the ghost real estate agent say to the ghost?
"I'm sorry, Sir, we have nothing suitable for you to haunt at the moment."

What is a ghost's favorite Wild West town?
Tombstone.

Why did the ghosts hold a seance?
To try to contact the living.

Which weight do ghosts box at?
Phantom weight.

What's the first thing a ghost does when it gets into the front seat of a car?
Fasten the sheet belt.

Mrs Monster to Mr Monster: "Try to be nice to my mother when she visits us this weekend, dear. Fall down when she hits you."

How does a witch tell the time?
She wears a witch watch.

Why was Baron Frankenstein never lonely?
Because he was good at making fiends.

Mr Monster: "Oi, hurry up with my supper."
Mrs Monster: "Oh, do be quiet – I've only got three pairs of hands."

1st Ghost: "Am I late for dinner?"
2nd Ghoul: "Yes, everyone's been eaten."

Father monster: "Johnny, don't make faces at that man. I've told you before not to play with your food."

1st Ghoulish Fiend: "I had a nice man to dinner last night."
2nd Ghoulish Fiend: "So you enjoyed having him?"
1st Ghoulish Fiend: "Oh, yes, he was delicious."

What do you get if you cross a yeti with a kangaroo?
A fur coat with big pockets.

Waiter on ocean liner: "Would you like the menu, Sir?"
Monster: "No thanks, just bring me the passenger list."

What do you get if you cross an elephant with the abominable snowman?
A jumbo yeti.

What do you call two witches who share a room?
Broom-mates.

Why did the witch put her broom in the washing machine?
She wanted a clean sweep.

What noise does a witch's breakfast cereal make?
Snap, cackle, pop!

"Doctor, doctor, I think I'm a witch!"
"You'd better lie down for a spell."

Witch: "I'd like a new frog, please."
Pet Shop Assistant: "But you bought one only yesterday. What happened?"
Witch: "It Kermit-ted suicide."

NEEP!!
NEEP!

Witch in shoe shop: "I'd like a pair of sandals, please."
Shop Assistant: "Certainly, madam, what kind?"
Witch: "Open-toed, of course."

What do you call a wizard from outer space?
A flying sorcerer.

What do you call a motor bike belonging to a witch?
A brrooooom stick.

Why do skeletons drink milk?
Because it's good for the bones.

Why did Mr and Mrs Werewolf call their son Camera?
Because he was always snapping.

Why shouldn't you grab a werewolf by its tail?
It might be the werewolf's tail, but it could be the end
of you.

Was Dracula ever married?
No, he was a bat-chelor.

Why was Dracula so happy at the races?
His horse won by a neck.

What do you get if you cross a vampire with Al
Capone?
A fangster!

How does a vampire enter his house?
Through the bat flap.

Why are skeletons usually so calm?
Nothing gets under their skin.

What do you call a skeleton who's always telling lies?
A bony phoney.

What do vampires gamble with?
Stake money.

How did skeletons send each other letters in the days
of the Wild West?
By Bony Express.

What do you get if you cross a vampire with a mummy?
A flying bandage.

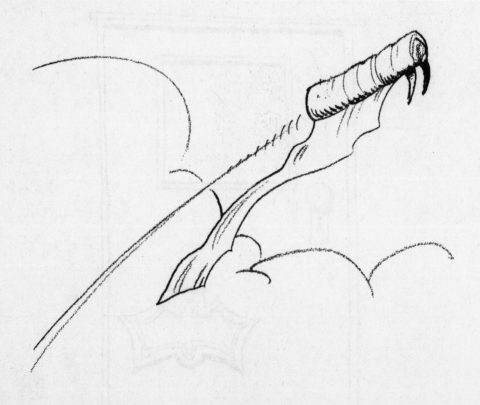

What sort of group do vampires join?
A blood group.

Who has the most dangerous job in Transylvania?
Dracula's dentist.

Why was Dracula always willing to help young vampires?
Because he liked to see new blood in the business.

What happens to a witch when she loses her temper?
She flies off the handle.

Why do skeletons hate winter?
Because the cold goes right through them.

How can you tell if a vampire has been at your tomato juice?
By the teeth-marks on the lid.

What do you get if you cross a vampire with a car?
A monster that attacks vehicles and sucks out all their petrol.

What do you call an old and foolish vampire?
A silly old sucker.

How does a vampire get through life with only one fang?
He has to grin and bare it.

What is Count Dracula's favorite pudding?
Leeches and scream.

If a boxer was knocked out by Dracula, what would he be?
Out for the Count.

Who is a vampire likely to fall in love with?
The girl necks door.

What is red, sweet and bites people in the neck?
A jampire.

What's it called when a vampire kisses you good-night?
Necking.

Mrs Vampire: "Will you still love me when I'm old and ugly?"
Mr Vampire: "Darling, of course I do."

What's the difference between a vampire with toothache and a rainstorm?
One roars with pain and the other pours with rain.

What is Dracula's favorite breed of dog?
The bloodhound.

Why did the vampire actress turn down so many film offers?
She was waiting for a part she could get her teeth into.

What do you get if you cross a midget with Dracula?
A vampire that sucks blood from your kneecaps.

What do you get if you cross an owl with a vampire?
A bird that's ugly but doesn't give a hoot.

Did you hear about the doctor who crossed a parrot
with a vampire?
It bit his neck, sucked his blood and said, "Who's a
pretty boy then?"

What's a vampire's worst enemy?
Fang decay.

What is bright red and dumb?
A blood clot.

How do you make a vampire float?
Take two scoops of ice-cream, a glass of Coke and
add one vampire.

1st Vampire: "I don't think much of your sister's neck."
2nd Vampire: "Never mind – eat the vegetables instead."

What is ugly, scary and very blue?
A vampire holding his breath.

A man was walking behind a hearse with a big vampire's cat on a lead. Behind them stretched a long line of mourners. "What happened?" asked a passer-by.
"The vampire's cat bit my wife, and she died of fright."
"Can I borrow it?" the passer-by asked.
The man pointed behind him "Get in the queue," he said.

What do you get if you cross a vampire with a flea?
Lots of very worried dogs.

What do you call a vampire with a car on his head?
Jack.

Father: "I want to take my girl out of this terrible math class."
Teacher: "But she's top of the class."
Father: "That's why I think it must be a terrible class."

Girl: "Mom, you know you're always worried about me failing math?"
Mother: "Yes."
Girl: "Well, your worries are over."

Mother: "Did you get a good place in the geography test?"
Daughter: "Yes, Mom, I sat next to the cleverest kid in the class."

Father: "This report gives you a D for conduct and an A for courtesy. How on earth did you manage that?"
Son: "Easy. Whenever I punch someone, I apologize."

"It's a note from the teacher about me telling lies – but it's not true."

Wife to Husband: "I think Spencer may grow up to be a space scientist. I was talking to his teacher today and she said he was taking up space."

Girl: "My teacher's a peach."
Mother: "You mean she's sweet."
Girl: "No, she has a heart of stone."

Teacher to pupil: "How many thousand times have I told you not to exaggerate?"

Boy: "Why did you throw my homework in the bin?"
Teacher: "Because it was rubbish."

Jennifer: "How come you did so badly in history? I thought you had all the dates written on your sleeve?"
Miriam: "That's the trouble, I put on my geography blouse by mistake."

Why don't astronauts get hungry after being blasted into space?
Because they've just had a big launch.

Teacher: "How many make a dozen?"
Boy: "12."
Teacher: "Correct. And how many make a million?"
Boy: "Dad says very few."

Headmaster: "I've called you into my office, Peter, because I want to talk to you about two words I wish you wouldn't use so often. One is 'great' and the other is 'lousy.'"
Peter: "Certainly Sir. What are they?"

Teacher: "Colin, one of your essays is very good but the other one I can't read."
Colin: "Yes, sir. My mother is a much better writer than my father."

Mother: "How was your first day at school?"
Little Boy: "Okay, but I haven't got my present yet."
Mother: "What do you mean?"
Little Boy: "Well the teacher gave me a chair, and said, 'Sit there for the present.'"

What did the little eye say to the big eye?
"Aye, aye, Captain!"

A country lad was being interviewed for a farm
laborer's job.
"You must be fit," said the farmer. "Have you had any
illnesses?"
"No, sir," said the lad.
"Any accidents?"
"No, sir."
"But you walked in here on crutches," said the farmer.
"Surely you must have had an accident?"
"Oh that!" replied the lad. "Oi were tossed by a bull –
but it weren't no accident, sir. He did it on purpose!"

Two Irishmen bought two horses at a sale in County
Cork. Both the horses were similar, so Pat said to
Mike, "How shall we tell which horse is whose?"
"Oi tell you what," said Mike, "we'll bob the tail of one
of them." But by a mistake the tails of both horses
were bobbed, so they were still in the same
predicament.
"Oi know the answer," said Pat. "You take the white
one, and I'll take the black one!"

What do you get if you cross a skunk and an owl?
A bird that smells but doesn't give a hoot!

What do you get if you cross a cow and a camel?
Lumpy milkshakes!

What do you get if you cross a sheep-dog and a bunch
of daisies?
Collie-flowers!

What do you get if you cross an elephant and peanut-
butter?
Either peanut-butter that never forgets, or an elephant
that sticks to the roof of your mouth.

What do you get if you cross a zebra and a donkey?
A zeedonk.

What do you get if you cross a kangaroo and a mink?
A fur jumper with pockets.

What do you get if you cross a sheep and a rainstorm?
A wet blanket.

What do you get if you cross a centipede and a parrot?
A walkie-talkie.

How do you make gold soup?
Use fourteen carats.

How do pixies eat?
By gobblin.

Why did the orange stop rolling down the hill?
It ran out of juice.

Who makes suits and eats spinach?
Popeye the Tailorman.

If King Kong went to Hong Kong to play ping-pong and
died, what would they put on his coffin?
A lid.

"Why are you taking that steel wool home?"
"I'm going to knit myself a car."

Did you hear about the stupid water-polo player?
His horse drowned...

Did you hear about the stupid tap dancer?
He fell in the sink.

Where does Tarzan buy his clothes?
At a Jungle Sale.

What lives in a pod and is a Kung Fu expert?
Bruce Pea.

What's big, hairy and can fly?
King Koncorde.

What do cannibal children like playing best?
Swallow my leader.

What kind of cans are there in Mexico?
Mexicans.

What is a mermaid?
A deep-she fish.

What is yellow and goes click-click?
A ball-point banana.

Have you heard the joke about the wall?
You'd never get over it.

What can you make that can't be seen?
A noise.

What has four eyes and a mouth?
The Mississippi.

A little thing, a pretty thing, without a top or bottom.
What am I?
A diamond ring.

How do you get rid of varnish?
Take away the R.

What fish do dogs chase?
Catfish.

If a crocodile makes shoes, what does a banana make?
Slippers.

What is it that even the most careful person overlooks?
His nose.

What is a tornado?
Mother Nature doing the twist.

What pet makes the loudest noise?
A trum-pet.

What key went to college?
A Yale.

What is full of holes but can hold water?
A sponge.

What makes the Tower of Pisa lean?
It doesn't eat much.

How many days of the week start with the letter T?
Four: Tuesday, Thursday, today and tomorrow.

Will you remember me in one day's time?
Of course I will.
Will you remember me in a week's time?
Of course I will.
Will you remember me in a year's time?
Of course I will.
Will you remember me in ten years' time?
Of course I will.
Knock, knock.
Who's there?
See – you've forgotten already!

Knock, knock.
Who's there?
Olive.
Olive who?
Olive across the road.

Knock, knock.
Who's there?
Fanny.
Fanny who?
Fanny the way you keep saying "Who's there?"

244

Knock, knock.
Who's there?
Little old lady.
Little old lady who?
I didn't know you could yodel.

Knock, knock.
Who's there?
Howard.
Howard who?
Howard you like to stand out here in the cold while some idiot keeps saying "who's there....?"

A snobbish woman was showing a friend round her new home.
"It's very lovely," her friend admitted, "but what you need in this big room is a chandelier."
"I know, my dear" said her gracious hostess, "but nobody in the family plays one."

"I'll lend you a dollar if you promise not to keep it too long."
"Oh, I won't. I'll spend it right away."

Auntie Gladys bought herself a new rear-engine continental car. She took an old friend for a spin, but after only half a mile, the car broke down. Both women got out and opened up the front of the car.

"Oh, Gladys," said her friend, "you've lost your engine!"

"Never mind, dear," said Auntie, "I've got a spare one in the trunk."

"Is this a second-hand shop?"

"Yes, sir."

"Good. Can you fit one on my watch, please?"

An angry woman went into the butcher's shop and snapped, "That joint you sold me was awful!"

"Why, madam, was it tough?" asked the butcher.

"Tough!" said the woman. "I should say it was. Why, I couldn't even get my fork into the gravy!"

"Why are you laughing?"

"My silly dentist just pulled one of my teeth out."

"I don't see much to laugh about in that."

"Ah, but it was the wrong one!"

"Are you superstitious?"

"No."

"Then lend me $13".

"In the park this morning I was surrounded by lions."
"Lions! In the park?"
"Yes – dandelions!"

"How's your business coming along?"
"I'm looking for a new cashier."
"But you only had a new one last week."
"That's the one I'm looking for."

"Can I borrow that book of yours – *How To Become A Millionaire*?"
"Sure. Here you are."
"Thanks – but half the pages are missing."
"What's the matter? Isn't half a million enough for you?"

"My brother's been practising the violin for ten years."
"Is he any good?"
"No. It was nine years before he found out he wasn't supposed to blow it."

As a passer-by was walking under a ladder, a brick fell from a hod and hit him on the head, ruining his new bowler. He looked up at the hod-carrier and shouted, "You clumsy great oaf! One of those bricks hit me!"
"You're lucky," came the reply. "Look at all the ones that didn't!"

"A pound of kiddies, please, butcher."
"You mean a pound of kidneys."
"That's what I said, diddie I?"

A man sitting in a barber's chair noticed that the barber's hands were very dirty. When he commented on this, the barber explained, "Yes sir, no one's been in for a shampoo yet."

"Have you any invisible ink?"
"Certainly, sir. What color?"

An extremely tall man with round shoulders, very long arms and one leg six inches shorter than the other went into a tailor's shop.
"I'd like to see a suit that will fit me," he told the tailor.
"So would I, sir," the tailor sympathized. "So would I."

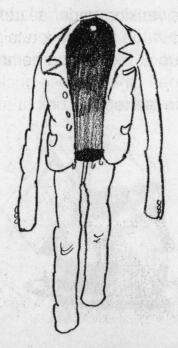

Harry was telling his friend about his holiday in Switzerland. His friend had never been to Switzerland, and asked, "What did you think of the scenery?"
"Oh, I couldn't see much," Harry admitted. "There were all those mountains in the way."

"What did you get for Christmas?"
"A mouth-organ. It's the best present I ever got."
"Why?"
"My mom gives me ten cents a week not to blow it."

"What sort of a car has your dad got?"
"I can't remember the name. I think it starts with T."
"Really? Ours only starts with gas."

"What do you mean by telling everyone I'm an idiot?"
"I'm sorry. I didn't know it was supposed to be a secret."

At the scene of a bank raid the policeman came running up to the officer and said, "He got away, sir!"
The officer was furious. "But I told you to put a man on all the exits!" he roared. "How could he have got away?"
"He left by one of the entrances, sir!"

"Good morning, sir. I'm applying for the job as handyman."

"I see. Well, are you handy?"

"Couldn't be more so. I only live next door."

A policeman discovered a suspicious-looking character lolling up against a doorway.

"What are you doing here?" the officer demanded.

"I live here," said the man. "I've lost my front door key."

"Well, ring the bell, then," said the policeman.

"Oh, I did ten minutes ago."

"Perhaps there's no one in then," suggested the officer.

"Oh yes, my wife and two children are in."

"So why not ring again."

"No," said the man. "let 'em wait!"

"What do you think of this photograph of me?"

"It makes you look older, frankly."

"Oh well, it'll save the cost of having another one taken later on."

Notice (in a new shop window): Don't go elsewhere and be robbed – try us!

"Do you like my new cap?"

"Yes, very nice."

"I used to wear a pork-pie hat, but the gravy kept running down my ears..."

A very shy young man went into an optician's one day to order a new pair of spectacles. Behind the counter was an extremely pretty young girl, the sight of which reduced the customer to total confusion.

"Can I help you, sir?" she asked with a ravishing smile.

"Er – yes – er – I want a pair of rim-speckled hornicles...I mean I want a pair of heck-rimmed spornicles...er...I mean..."

At which point the optician himself came to the rescue.

"It's all right, Miss Jones. What the gentleman wants is a pair of rim-sporned hectacles."

An old lady was considering buying a squirrel fur coat.

"But will it be all right in the rain?" she asked anxiously.

"Oh certainly, madam," said the manager smoothly. "After all, you've never seen a squirrel with an umbrella have you?"

A man went into a tailor's shop and saw a man hanging by one arm from the center of the ceiling.

"What's he doing there?" he asked the tailor.

"Oh, pay no attention," said the tailor, "he thinks he's a lightbulb."

"Well, why don't you tell him he isn't?" asked the startled customer.

"What?" replied the tailor, "and work in the dark?"

"My brother's just opened a shop."

"Really? How's he doing?"

"Six months. He opened it with a crowbar."

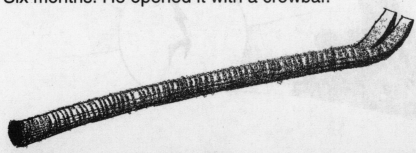

At a party, a conjurer was producing egg after egg
from a little boy's ear.
"There!" he said proudly. "I bet your Mom can't
produce eggs without hens, can she?"
"Oh yes, she can," said the boy, "she keeps ducks."

"Have you ever seen a duchess?"
"Yes – it's the same as an English 's'!"

Jennifer: "Are you coming to my party?"
Sandra: "No, I ain't going."
Jennifer: "Now, you know what Miss told us. Not ain't.
It's I am not going, he is not going, she is not going,
they are not going."
Sandra: "Blimey, ain't nobody going?"

This match won't light.
That's funny – it did this morning.

A noise woke me up this morning.
What was that?
The crack of dawn.

"It can't go on! It can't go on!"
"What can't go on?"
"This baby's vest – it's too small for me."

"It's gone forever – gone forever I tell you."
"What has?"
"Yesterday."

At a concert, the boring singer with the tuneless voice
announced,
"I should now like to sing 'Over The Hills and Far Away.'"
"Thank goodness for that," whispered someone in the
audience. "I thought he was going to stay all evening."

A stupid man was struggling out of his house with a big
table. His neighbor said to him, "Hello, Harry. Where
are you going with that then?"
And Harry replied, "I'm taking it to the draper's shop to
have it measured for a new tablecloth."

As the judge said to the dentist: "Do you swear to pull
the tooth, the whole tooth, and nothing but the tooth?"

"They're not going to grow bananas any longer."
"Really? Why not?"
"Because they're long enough already."

"Just think – a big chocolate ice-cream, a bag of scrumptious toffees, and a seat at the cinema for ten cents."
"Did you get all that for ten cents?"
"No – but just think...!"

"I wonder where I got that puncture?"
"Maybe it was at that last fork in the road..."

As two boys were passing the vicarage, the vicar leaned over the wall and showed them a ball. "Is this yours?" he asked.
"Did it do any damage, vicar?" said one of the boys.
"No," replied the vicar.
"Then it's mine."

A man in a swimming pool was on the very top diving-board. He poised, lifted his arms, and was about to dive when the attendant came running up, shouting, "Don't dive – there's no water in that pool!"
"That's all right," said the man. "I can't swim!"

254

"My uncle's got a wooden leg."
"That's nothing. My auntie has a wooden chest."

Did you hear about the girl who got engaged to a chap and then found out he had a wooden leg? She broke it off, of course...

"I bet I can make you speak like a Red Indian."
"How?"
"That's right!"

Passer-by (to fisherman): "Is this river any good for fish?"
Fisherman: "It must be. I can't get any of them to leave it."

Vegetarian: "I've lived on nothing but vegetables for years."
Bored listener: "That's nothing. I've lived on Earth all my life."

"Waiter, waiter, there's a bird in my soup."
"That's all right, sir. It's bird-nest soup."

"Waiter, waiter, your tie is in my soup!"
"That's all right, sir. It's not shrinkable."

"Waiter, waiter, this coffee tastes like mud."
"I'm not surprised, sir, it was ground only a few minutes ago."

"Waiter, waiter, does the pianist play requests?"
"Yes, sir"
"Then ask him to play tiddlywinks until I've finished my meal."

There was a young man from Quebec
Who wrapped both his legs round his neck!
But then he forgot
How to undo the knot,
And now he's an absolute wreck!

There once was a writer named Wright,
Who instructed his son to write right;
He said, "Son, write Wright right.
It's not right to write
Wright as 'rite' – try to write Wright all right!"

A charming young singer named Hannah,
Got caught in a flood in Savannah;
As she floated away,
Her sister, they say,
Accompanied her on the piannah!

"You've got your socks on inside out."
"I know, Mom, but there are holes on the other side."

"Dad, is an ox a sort of male cow?"
"Sort of, yes."
"And equine means something to do with horses,
doesn't it?"
"That's right."
"So what's an equinox?"

At the seaside, Mom waxed all lyrical at the beauty of
the sunset over the sea.
"Doesn't the sun look wonderful setting on to the
horizon?" she breathed.
"Yes," said young Sammy, "and there won't half be a
fizz when it touches the water!"

"Dad, what are all the holes in the new garden shed?"
"They're knot-holes."
"What do you mean 'they're not holes'? I can put my finger into them."

"How did your mom know you hadn't washed your face?"
"I forgot to wet the soap."

"My brother's one of the biggest stick-up men in town."
"Gosh, is he really?"
"Yes, he's a six-foot-six bill-poster."

Dotty Aunt Muriel received a letter one morning, and upon reading it burst into floods of tears. "What's the matter?" asked her companion.
"Oh dear," sobbed Auntie, "It's my favorite nephew. He's got three feet."
"Three feet?" exclaimed her friend. "Surely that's not possible?"
"Well," said Auntie, "his mother's just written to tell me he's grown another foot!"

"Come on, Charles, I'll take you to the zoo."
"If the zoo wants me, let them come and get me!"

...ne with a pain in his stomach.
..... your tea," said his mother. "Your
..... because it's empty. It'll be alright
when you've got something in it." Shortly afterwards
Dad came in from the office, complaining of a
headache.

"That's because it's empty," said his bright son, "You'd
be all right if you had something in it."

"My Uncle Ben and Aunt Flo haven't had a row for five
years."
"That's wonderful."
"Not really. Uncle Ben lives in China."

Visitor: "You're very quiet, Jennifer."
Jennifer: "Well, my mom gave me 10 cents not to say
anything about your red nose."

"Mom, can I have two pieces of cake, please?"
"Certainly – take this piece and cut it in two!"

"Dad, when I get old will the calves of my legs be
cows?"

"Don't eat the biscuits so fast – they'll keep."
"I know, but I want to eat as many as I can before I
lose my appetite."

"You youngsters are soft an[d]
your age I got up at six o'c[lock]
walked five or six miles be[fore]
think nothing of it."
"I don't blame you, Grandpa. I wouldn't think much of it myself."

After a visit to the circus, Geoff and Don were discussing the thrills and marvels they had seen. "I didn't think much of the knife-thrower, did you?" said Geoff.
"I thought he was super!" enthused Don.
"Well I didn't," said Geoff. "He kept chucking those knives at that soppy girl and didn't hit her once!"

Trevor came rushing in to his Dad.
"Dad," he puffed, "is it true that an apple a day keeps the doctor away?"
"That's what they say," said his Dad.
"Well, give us an apple quick – I've just broken the doctor's window!"

"Mom, you know that vase that's been handed down from generation to generation?"
"Yes."
"Well, this generation's dropped it."

Mom: "Sue, there were two chocolate cakes in the larder yesterday, and now there's only one. Why?"
Sue: "I don't know. It must have been so dark I didn't see the other one."

Mom: "Jackie, go outside and play with your whistle. Your father can't read his paper."
Jackie: "Wow, I'm only eight, and I can read it!"

Helen: "Mom, do you know what I'm going to give you for your birthday?"
Mom: "No, dear, what?"
Helen: "A nice teapot."
Mom: "But I've got a nice teapot."
Helen: "No you haven't. I've just dropped it!"

Little girl, having been sent to get the morning milk in: "Mom, the milkman's been and gone and not come!"

Little George was crying one day, and his dad asked him why. "I've lost five cents," sobbed George.
"Never mind," said his dad kindly. "Here's five more for you." At which George howled louder than ever. "Now what is it?" asked his dad.
"I wish I'd said I'd lost ten cents!"

"Mom! There's a man at the door collecting for the Old Folks' Home. Shall I give him Grandma?"

A certain little boy had been spanked by his father one morning.
When his dad came in from the office that evening, the boy called out sulkily,
"Mom! Your husband's just come home."

Did you hear about the little boy who was named after his father? They called him Dad.

Mom: "Jimmy, where are you off to now?"
Jimmy: "I'm going to join the army."
Mom: "But legally you're only an infant."
Jimmy: "That's all right. I'm going to join the infantry."

Teddy came thundering down the stairs, much to his father's annoyance.
"Teddy," he called, "how many more times have I got to tell you to come downstairs quietly? Now, go back upstairs and come down like a civilized human being."
There was a silence, and Teddy reappeared in the front room.
"That's better," said his father. "Now in future will you always come down the stairs like that."
"Suits me," said Teddy. "I slid down the bannister."

"Giles, we're having very important guests for lunch today, so clean yourself up and make yourself presentable, please."
"Why – they're not going to eat me, are they?"

"Now then, Deirdre, eat up all your greens like a good girl. They're good for your complexion, you know."
"But I don't want to have a green complexion!"

Teacher: "What's this a picture of?"
Class: "Don't know, Miss."
Teacher: "It's a kangaroo."
Class: "What's a kangaroo, Miss?"
Teacher: "A kangaroo is a native of Australia."
Smallest boy: "Wow, my sister's married one of them!"

How many drops of acetic acid does it take to make a stink bomb?
Quite a phew.

"Why did you come back early from your holidays?" one of Alec's friends asked him.
"Well, on the first day we were there one of the chickens died and that night we had chicken soup. The next day one of the pigs died and we had pork chops..."
"But why did you come back early?"
"Well, on the third day the farmer's father-in-law died. What would you have done?"

The chemistry teacher added acid from one beaker to a solution in another. Within seconds the classroom was filled with foul-smelling smoke that bubbled out of the beaker.

"Now, boys," he spluttered, "I'm going to drop this one dollar coin into the beaker. Will the coin dissolve in the acid?" And as he spoke he plopped the coin into the foaming beaker.

"It definitely won't dissolve, sir!" said one boy.

"How can you be so sure?" asked the teacher.

"Because if it would, you would have never dropped it into the beaker."

"You boy!" called a policeman. "Can you help? We're looking for a man with a huge red nose called Cotters..."

"Really?" said the boy. "What're his ears called?"

"Can I have some two-handed cheese, please?" a man in a restaurant asked the waiter.

"What do you mean 'two-handed cheese'?" asked the waiter.

"The kind you eat with one hand and hold your nose with the other."

"What's your new perfume called?" a young man asked his girlfriend.

"High Heaven," she replied.

"I asked what it was called, not what it smells to!"

264

A blind man went into a shop, picked up his dog by the tail and swung it around his head. "Can I help you?" asked the assistant.

"No thanks," said the blind man, "I'm just looking around."

Which soldiers smell of salt and pepper?
Seasoned troopers.

"Five dollars for one question!" said the woman to the fortune teller.
"That's very expensive, isn't it?"
"Next!"

"I'm sorry," said the surgeon. "But I left a sponge in you when I operated last week."
"Oh," said the patient, "I was wondering why I was so thirsty all the time."

"What do you do?" a young man asked the beautiful girl he was dancing with.
"I'm a nurse."
"I wish I could be ill and let you nurse me," he whispered in her ear.
"That would be miraculous. I work on the maternity ward."

There were two mosquitoes watching blood donors giving their blood. "It's not fair," said one to the other. "They're happy to lie down and let someone drain a pint of blood, but if we zoomed down for a quick nip, they'd do their best to kill us."

What's green, has four legs and two trunks?
Two seasick tourists.

"I'm suffering from bad breath."
"You should do something about it!"
"I did. I just sent my wife to the dentist."

"I'd like a cheap parrot, please," an old lady said to a pet shop owner.
"This one's cheap and it sings 'God Save The Queen.'"
"Never mind that," said the customer, "Is it tender?"

"What's the matter?" one man asked another.
"My wife left me when I was in the bath last night," sobbed the second man.
"She must have been waiting for years for the chance," replied the first.

Why is perfume obedient?
Because it is scent wherever it goes.

eat raw fish and

too if you had to eat

es in here."

have new ones by

"What's the secret of living to be 100?" the reporter asked the old man.
"Slugs!" replied the centenarian.
"Slugs?"
"Yes! I've never eaten one in my entire life!"

"There's a dreadful smell of BO in here," said the new office-boy. "It's the automatic air-conditioning," said his boss.
"Automatic air-conditioning?"
"Yes! Whenever the weather gets hot it automatically breaks down!"

"The walls in my flat are very thin," a young girl complained to her friend.
"You mean you can hear everything that's going on next door?"
"Not just that: when they peel onions I start to cry!"

267

An elephant ran away from a circus and ended up in a little old lady's back garden. Now she had never seen an elephant before, so she rang the police.
"Please come quickly," she said to the policeman who answered the phone. "There's a strange looking animal in my garden picking up cabbages with its tail."
"What's it doing with them?" asked the policeman.
"If I told you," said the old lady, "You'd never believe me!"

"Doctor, doctor, my baby's swallowed a watch!"
"Give it some Epsom Salts: that should help it pass the time."

A very fat lady got on a crowded bus. "Is no one going to give me a seat?" she boomed. A very small man stood up and said, "I'll make a small contribution."

Doctor: "I can't diagnose the cause of your bad breath. I think it must be the drink."
Patient: "Okay, I'll come back when you're sober."

Two caterpillars were crawling along a twig when a butterfly flew by. "You know," said one caterpillar to the other, "When I grow up, you'll never get me in one of those things."

268

Three animals were having a drink in a cafe, when the owner asked for the money.

"I'm not paying," said the duck. "I've only got one bill and I'm not breaking it."

"I've spent my last buck," said the deer.

"Then the duck'll *have* to pay," said the skunk. "Getting here cost me my last scent!"

A blind man was waiting to cross the road when a dog stopped and cocked its leg against him. The blind man felt in his pocket for a sweet, bent down, and offered it to the dog. A passer-by remarked what a very kind act that was considering what the dog had just done.

"Not at all," said the blind man. "I only wanted to find out which end to kick."

A man with BO walked into a drugstore and said, "I'd like something to take this smell away."

"So would I, sir," said the chemist. "So would I."

Did you hear about the man with grease stains all over his jacket?

He had a chip on his shoulder.

What illness did everyone on the Enterprise catch?

Chicken Spocks.

A punk walked into a barber's shop and sat in an empty chair. "Haircut, sir?" asked the barber.
"No, just change the oil please!"

The food at the club dinner was awful. The soup tasted like dishwater, the fish was off, the meat was overcooked, the vegetables were obviously old. The last straw for one member was the custard which was thick and lumpy.
"This meal is disgusting!" he roared. "And what's more, I'm going to bring it up at the AGM next week!"

Did you hear about the new prize for people who cure themselves of BO?
It's called the No-Smell Prize.

"Doctor, doctor! Every time I drink a cup of tea I get a sharp pain in by nose."
"Have you tried taking the spoon out of the cup?"

"Doctor, doctor, I've just been sprayed by a skunk. Should I put some cream on it?"
"Well you could. But I doubt if you'll be able to catch it."

What's black and white, pongs and hangs from a line?
A drip-dry skunk.

"I'm very worried about my little boy's nail biting habit,"
a woman said to her doctor.
"Nail biting is very common in youngsters," said the
doctor.
"What! Six-inch rusty ones?"

"You've got the worst BO I've ever smelt," said the
doctor. "You need a major operation."
"I'd like a second opinion, please."
So the doctor sniffed and said, "You've got the worst
BO I've ever smelt. You need a major operation!"

"Did you hear about the snake with a bad cold?"
"No! Tell me about the snake with a bad cold."
"It had to viper nose."

What dog smells of onions?
A hot dog.

Hotel guest: "Can you give me a room and a bath, please?"
Porter: "I can give you a room, but you'll have to bath yourself."

"Ugh! You smell terrible," said a doctor to a patient.
"That's odd," said the patient, "That's what the other doctor said."
"If you were told that by another doctor, why have you come to me?"
"Because I wanted a second opinion."

"Doctor, doctor, my friend told me I had BO."
"And what makes you think he's right, you disgusting, smelly, malodorous, foul, little man?"

"Why's your son crying?" the doctor asked a young woman in his surgery.
"He has four baked beans stuck up his nose."
"And why's his little sister screaming?"
"She wants the rest of her lunch back."

During the French Revolution a Frenchman, an Englishman and an Irishman were condemned to the guillotine. The Frenchman was called first and he very calmly put his head on the block. The executioner released the blade, but halfway down it stuck. The tradition in France was that if this happened, the condemned man was set free. So the Frenchman was saved.

When the Englishman laid his head on the block, the executioner released the blade. The same thing happened, so he was released.

The Irishman was led from the cart, kicking and screaming, "I'm not going near that thing until you get it fixed!"

"Those currant buns you sold me yesterday had three cockroaches in them," a woman complained over the phone to a baker.

"Sorry about that," said the baker. "If you bring the cockroaches back I'll give you the three currants I owe you."

What lies on the ground 100 feet up in the air and smells?

A dead centipede.

An irate customer in a restaurant complained that his fish was bad, so the waiter picked it up, smacked it and said, "Naughty, naughty, naughty!"

A man with a newt on his shoulder walked into a pub.
"What do you call him," asked the barmaid. "Tiny," said
the man.
"Why do you call him Tiny?"
"Because he's my newt!"

There was a little old lady from a small town in
America who had to go to Texas. She was amazed at
the size of her hotel and her suite. She went into the
huge cafe and said to the waitress, who took her order
for a cup of coffee, that she had never before seen
anything as big as the hotel or her suite.
"Everything's big in Texas, ma'am," said the waitress.
The coffee came in the biggest cup the old lady had
ever seen.
"I told you, ma'am, that everything is big in Texas,"
said the waitress.
On her way back to the suite, the lady got lost in the
vast corridors. She opened the door of a darkened
room and fell into an enormous swimming pool.
"Please!" she screamed. "Don't flush it!"

Why did the stupid racing driver make ten pit stops
during the Grand Prix?
He was asking for directions.

A man walked into a bar holding a cow pat in his hand.
"Look everyone," he cried. "See what I almost stood
on!"

Two cannibals were having lunch.
"Your wife makes a great soup," said one to the other.
"Yes!" agreed the first. "But I'm going to miss her terribly."

"Do you know the difference between roast chicken and a long, lingering kiss?" a boss asked his secretary one day.
"No, I don't," she said.
"Great!" said the boss. "Let's have chicken for lunch."

What's wet, smells and goes ba-bump, ba-bump?
A skunk in the spin-drier.

How do you keep an imbecile happy all his life?
Tell him a joke when he's a baby.

There was a little boy who had really smelly feet. One night before he went to bed his mother told him that tomorrow was a very special day and that when he woke up his feet wouldn't smell at all. The boy was so excited he hardly slept. But, eventually, he dropped off. Next morning his mother woke him early. The first thing he did was to sniff his feet. They smelled even worse than before.
His mother just laughed and said, "April Fool!"

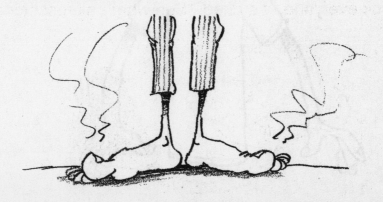

What do you call a man with cow droppings all over his shoes?
An incowpoop.

What did the grape do when the elephant sat on it?
It let out a little wine.

Why do grape harvesters have noses?
So they have something to pick during the growing season.

What do you get if you cross a nun and a chicken?
A pecking order.

Did you hear about the man who had BO on one side only?
He bought Right Guard, but couldn't find any Left Guard.

"Mommy! Mommy! Have you seen my Cabbage Patch Doll?
"Shut up and finish your coleslaw!"

Why didn't the banana snore?
'Cos it was afraid to wake up the rest of the bunch.

Who is the biggest gangster in the sea?
Al Caprawn.

What does Luke Skywalker shave with?
A laser blade.

What do frogs drink?
Croaka Cola.

Who is in cowboy films and is always broke?
Skint Eastwood.

What's the fastest thing in water?
A motor-pike.

Where do snowmen go to dance?
A snowball.

Why did the idiot have his sundial floodlit?
So he could tell the time at night.

Which capital city cheats at exams?
Peking.

What do you call a flea that lives in an idiot's ear?
A space invader.

Why did the woman take a load of hay to bed?
To feed her nightmare.

What do cats prefer for breakfast?
Mice Crispies.

Did you hear about the Irish Kamikaze pilot?
He flew ninety-nine missions...

What do ants take when they are ill?
Antibiotics.

What's black and white and noisy?
A zebra with a drum-kit.

"Would you like a duck egg for tea?"
"Only if you 'quack' it for me."

An American tourist found himself in a sleepy English
village, and asked one of the locals the age of the
oldest inhabitant.
"Well, zur," replied the villager, "we bain't got one now.
He died last week."

A much traveled explorer was talking about the huge
mosquitoes of the African jungle.
"Were they vicious?" asked one of his listeners.
"No," replied the explorer casually, "they'd eat out of
your hand."

"I've just finished painting your portrait. There, don't
you think it looks like you?"
"Er...well...it probably looks better from a distance."
"I told you it was like you!"

A visitor to Ireland asked a farm laborer the time. "Sure, it's 12 o'clock, yer honor," answered the Irishman.
"Only 12?" queried the traveler. "I thought it was much later than that."
"Oh no, sir, it never gets later than that in these parts."
"How's that?"
"Well, sir, after 12 o'clock, it goes back to one."

One housewife had a kitchen so small that she could only use condensed milk.

"I saw six men standing under an umbrella and none of them got wet."
"Must have been a big umbrella."
"No. It wasn't raining."

"I've got a wonder watch. Only cost $2."
"What's a wonder watch?"
"Every time I look at it, I wonder if it's still going."

A tramp knocked at a door and asked for some food.
"Didn't I give you some pie a week ago?" asked the lady of the house.
"Yus, lady," said the tramp, "but I'm all right again now."

An old lady saw a little boy with a fishing-rod over his shoulder and a jar of tadpoles in his hand walking through the park one Sunday.

"Little boy," she called. "don't you know you shouldn't go fishing on a Sunday?"

"I'm not going fishing missus," he called back, "I'm going home."

"Farmer Giles, why do you have two barrels on your shotgun?"

"So that if I miss the fox with the first I can get him with the other."

"Why not fire with the other first, then?"

The new office-boy came into his boss's office and said, "I think you're wanted on the phone, sir."

"What d'you mean, you think?" demanded the boss.

"Well, sir, the phone rang, I answered it and a voice said 'Is that you, you old fool?' "

A man went into a police station and put a dead cat on the counter. "Somebody threw this into my front garden," he complained.

"Righto, sir," said the desk sergeant. "You come back in six months and if no one's claimed it, you keep it."

A tramp knocked on the back door of a house and asked for a bite to eat.

"Go away," said the lady of the house, "I never feed tramps."

"That's all right lady," said the tramp, "I'll feed myself."

An American tourist was visiting a quaint English village, and got talking to an old man in the local pub.
"And have you lived here all your life, sir?" asked the American.
"Not yet, m'dear," said the villager wisely.

"For our next Christmas dinner I'm going to cross a chicken with an octopus."
"What on earth for?"
"So we can all have a leg each."

Billy: "I never had a sledge when I was a kid. We were too poor."
Milly, feeling sorry for him: "What a shame! What did you do when it snowed?"
Billy: "Slid down the hills on my cousin."

Teacher: "I'd like to go through one whole day without having to punish you."
Girl: "You have my permission, Sir."

Father: "Jennifer, I've had a letter from your headmaster. It seems you've been neglecting your appearance."
Jennifer: "Dad?"
Father: "He says you haven't appeared in school all week."

Mother: "What did your father say about your report?"
Girl: "Well, if you want me to cut out the swear words, he didn't really say anything."

Teacher: "What happened to your homework?"
Boy: "I made it into a paper plane and someone hijacked it."

Teacher: "What's the best way to pass this geometry test?"
Boy: "Knowing all the angles?"

Boy: "Did you know the most intelligent kid in our class is deaf?"
Girl: "That's unfortunate."
Boy: "What did you say?"

Boy: "Where does the new kid come from?"
Girl: "Alaska."
Boy: "Don't bother – I'll ask her myself."

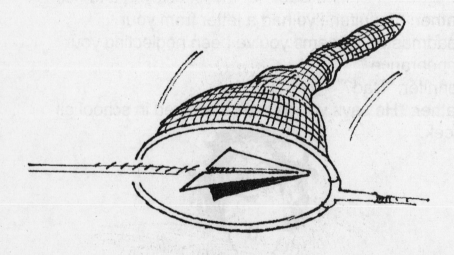

Tom: "Why are you scratching your head?"
Harry: "I've got those arithmetic bugs again."
Tom: "Arithmetic bugs – what are they?"
Harry: "Well, some people call them head lice."
Tom: "Then why do you call them arithmetic bugs?"
Harry: "Because they add to my misery, subtract from my pleasure, divide my attention and multiply like crazy."

Teacher: "What do you think astronauts wear to keep warm?"
Girl: "Apollo neck jumpers?"

Mother: "Why do you call your teacher 'Treasure'?"
Girl: "Because we wonder where she was dug up."

Teacher: "Why are you standing on your head?"
Boy: "I'm just trying to turn things over in my mind, sir."

Girl to Friend: "I'm sorry, I won't be able to come out tonight. I promised Dad that I would stay in and help him with my homework."

A hillbilly dragged his protesting son to a new school which had just opened in a nearby village. When they arrived, he took his son to see the headmaster.

"Howdy," said the hillbilly. "This here's my son Arthur. Now what kind of learnin' are you teachin'?"

"Oh, all the usual subjects," said the headmaster, nodding at the boy. "Reading, writing, arithmetic."

"What's this?" interrupted the father. "Arith... arith..What did you say?"

"Arithmetic, Sir," said the headmaster, instruction in geometry, algebra and trigonometry."

"Trigonometry!" cried the hillbilly. "That's what my boy needs. He's the worst darn shot in the family."

Why did Mickey Mouse take a trip to outer space?
He wanted to find Pluto.

What did the astronaut say to the author?
"I took your book into orbit and I couldn't put it down."

What happened when the wheel was invented?
It caused a revolution.

Did you hear about the mad scientist who put dynamite in his fridge?
They say he blew his cool

Ivan: "What are you reading?"
Andrea: "It's a book about electricity."
Ivan: "Oh, current events?"
Andrea: "No, light reading."

How did Benjamin Franklin discover electricity?
It came to him in a flash.

Where do geologists go for entertainment?
To rock concerts.

Why is history the sweetest lesson?
Because it's full of dates.

What's the difference between Noah's Ark and Joan of Arc?
One was made of wood and the other was Maid of Orleans.

Boy to Mother: "Our school cook really knows her new technology as well as her history. For school dinner today we had micro-chips with ancient grease."

Who conquered half the world, laying eggs along the way?
Attila the Hen.

Teacher: "Who can tell me what BC stands for?"
Girl: "Before calculators."

Girl: "Why do you call me pilgrim?"
Teacher: "Because you're making so little progress."

Father: "I see from your report that you're not doing so well in history. Why's this?"
Son: "I can't help it. He keeps asking me about things that happened before I was born."

Girl to Friend: "My mum is suffering from a minor neurosis. Every time she sees my report, she faints."

Why was Cleopatra so cantankerous?
She was Queen of Denial.

Boy to Friend: "My dad is so old, when he was at school, history was called current events."

A little boy came home from his first day at kindergarten and said to his mother:
"What's the use of going to school? I can't read, I can't write and the teacher won't let me talk."

Mother to Friend: "Karen's so imaginative! I asked her what the 'F' meant on her report, and she said 'fantastic.' "

Mother: "I told you not to eat cake before supper."
Daughter: "But Mum, it's part of my homework: 'If you take an eighth of a cake from a whole cake, how much is left?' "

Teacher: "Were you copying his sums?"
Girl: "No, Sir. I was just looking to see if he's got his right."

Teacher: "In this exam you will be allowed ten minutes for each question."
Boy: "How long is the answer?"

Teacher: "I told you to write this poem out 20 times because your handwriting is so bad."
Girl: "I'm sorry, Miss – my arithmetic's not that good either."

Teacher: "Why did you put that frog in Melinda's case?"
Boy: "Because I couldn't find a mouse."

Teacher: "Billy. Didn't you hear me call you?"
Billy: "Yes, Miss, but you told us yesterday not to answer back."

Mother: "What do you mean, the school must be haunted?"
Daughter: "Well, the headmaster kept going on about the school spirit."

What do you mean, my spelling isn't much good – that's my algebra.

A little boy went into a baker's. "How much are those cakes?" he asked.
"Two for 25 cents," said the baker. "How much does one cost?" asked the boy.
"13 cents," said the baker.
"Then I'll take the other one for 12 cents!" said the boy.

Teacher: "You should have been here at nine o'clock."
Boy: "Why? Did something happen?"

Teacher: "I wish you'd pay a little attention."
Girl: "I'm paying as little as possible."

Mother: "What did you learn at school today?"
Son: "Not enough. I have to go back tomorrow."

Mother: "Do you know a girl named Jenny Simon?"
Daughter: "Yes, she sleeps next to me in math."

Teacher: "If I had ten flies on my desk, and I swatted one, how many flies would be left?"
Girl: "One – the dead one!"

"I want to get married, vicar."
"So you want me to put the banns up?"
"No, we thought we'd just have a concertina after tea."

George had reached the age of 46, and not only was he still unmarried but he had never had a girlfriend.
"Come along now, George," said his father. "It's high time you got yourself a wife and settled down. Why, at your age I'd been married 20 years."
"But that was to Mom," said his son, "You can't expect me to marry a stranger!"

Harry was madly in love with Betty, but couldn't pluck up enough courage to pop the question face to face. Finally he decided to ask her on the telephone.
"Darling!" he blurted out, "will you marry me?"
"Of course, I will, you silly boy," she replied, "who is it speaking?"

Poor old Stephen sent his photograph off to a Lonely Hearts Club. They sent it back saying that they weren't that lonely.

Freddie had persuaded Amanda to marry him, and was formally asking her father for his permission. "Sir," he said, "I would like to have your daughter for my wife."
"Why can't she get one of her own?" said Amanda's father, disconcertingly.

On their first evening in their new home the bride went into the kitchen to fix the drinks. Five minutes later she came back into the living room in tears.
"What's the matter, my angel?" asked her husband anxiously.
"Oh Derek!" she sobbed, "I put the ice cubes in hot water to wash them and now they've disappeared!"

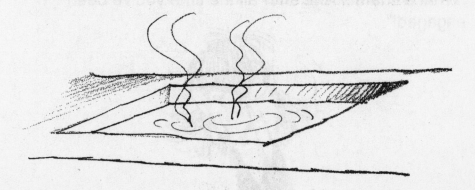

"Why aren't you married?"

"I was born that way."

Mrs Jones and her little daughter Karen were outside the church watching all the comings and goings of a wedding. After the photographs had been taken, everyone had driven off to the reception, and all the excitement was over Karen said to her mother "Why did the bride change her mind, Mommy?"

"How do you mean, change her mind?" asked Mrs Jones.

"Well," said the moppet, "she went into the church with one man and came out with another."

"Do you think, Professor, that my wife should take up the piano as a career?"

"No, I think she should put down the lid as a favor."

"Why did you refuse to marry Richard, Tessa?"

" 'Cos he said he would die if I didn't and I'm just curious."

"My Peter keeps telling everyone he's going to marry the most beautiful girl in the world."

"What a shame! And after all the time you've been engaged!"

"But she's so young to get married," sobbed Diana's mother. "Only seventeen!"
"Try not to cry about it," said her husband soothingly. "Think of it as not losing a daughter but as gaining a bathroom."

Rabbits can multipy – but only a snake can be an adder.

A huge lion was roaring through the jungle when he suddenly saw a tiny mouse. He stopped and snarled at it menacingly.
"You're very small," he growled fiercely.
"Well, I've been ill," replied the mouse piteously.

City boy (visiting country for the first time): "That farmer's a magician."
Country boy: "What – old Farmer Giles? How do you know?"
City boy: "He told me he was going to turn his cow into a field."

An angel in heaven was welcoming a new arrival.
"How did you get here?" he asked.
And the new angel replied, "flu..."

The proud owner of an impressive new clock was
showing it off to a friend. "This clock," he said, "will go
for 14 days without winding."
"Really," replied his friend. "And how long will it go if
you do wind it?"

So you want to play the banjo?
Why pick on that...?

A man stood up in a crowded restaurant and shouted,
"Anybody lost a roll of ten dollar notes with an elastic
band round them?"
There was a rush of people claiming to be the loser.
The first to arrive was an old tramp.
"Here you are," said the man, "I've found your elastic
band!"

A country lad on one of his rare visits to the market
town saw a music stool in the window of a shop. He
went in, bought it, and took it home. Two weeks later
he was back in the shop in a furious rage.
"Oi bin sittin' on this dratted stool for two weeks," he
told the manager, "an Oi ain't got a note out of it yet!"

A boastful American from Texas was being shown the sights of London by a taxi-driver. "What's that building there?" asked the Texan.

"That's the Tower of London, sir," replied the taxi-driver.

"Say, we can put up buildings like that in two weeks," drawled the Texan.

A little while later he said, "And what's that building we're passing now?"

"That's Buckingham Palace, sir, where the Queen lives."

"Is that so?" said the Texan, "Do you know back in Texas we could put a place like that up in a week?" A few minutes later they were passing Westminster Abbey. The American asked again, "Hey cabbie, what's that building over there?"

"I'm afraid I don't know, sir," replied the taxi-driver. "It wasn't there this morning!"

"Who was that at the door?"
"The Invisible Man."
"Tell him I can't see him."

Mean man: "How much for a haircut?"
Barber: "Forty cents."
Mean man: "How much for a shave?"
Barber: "Thirty cents."
Mean man: "Right – shave my head."

"Who was that at the door?"
"A man with a wooden leg."
"Tell him to hop it."

"Who was that at the door?"
"A man with a trumpet."
"Tell him to blow."

Two Irishmen were arranging to meet.
"If Oi get there first Oi'll put a chalk cross on the wall, Paddy."
"Roight ye are Mick," said Paddy. "And if Oi get there first, Oi'll rub it off."

"Vincent, why have you got a sausage stuck behind your ear?"
"Eh? Oh no, I must have eaten my pencil for lunch!"

At a restaurant which prided itself on its wide selection of dishes, a customer was inspecting the menu. "You'll find, sir," said the waiter proudly, "that everything is on the menu. Absolutely everything!"
"Yes, so I see," said the customer tartly, "so take it away and get me a clean one!"

"I went to see my doctor to see if he could help me give up smoking."
"What did he say?"
"He suggested that every time I felt like a smoke I should reach for a bar of chocolate."
"Did that do any good?"
"No – I can't get the chocolate to light."

298

The unluckiest man in the world: the deep sea diver coming up who met his ship going down.

Pete: "I haven't slept a wink for the past two nights."
Jimmy: "Why's that?"
Pete: "Granny broke her leg. The doctor put it in plaster and told her she shouldn't walk upstairs. You should hear the row when she climbs up the drainpipe."

"I like your Easter tie."
"Why do you call it my Easter tie?"
"It's got egg on it."

A man whose son had just passed his driving test went home one evening and found that the boy had driven slap into the sitting room. "How did you manage to do that?" he fumed.
"Quite simple, Dad. I came in through the kitchen and turned left!"

The dirty old tramp sidled up to a passer-by.
"Got a dollar for a bed for the night?" he muttered.
"No," said the passer-by firmly.
"Got 50 cents for a meal?"
"Certainly not."
"Oh....have you got 20 cents for a cup of tea, then?"
"No, I have not."
"Blimey – you'd better take my mouth-organ. You're worse off than I am!"

Did you hear about the Do-It-Yourself funeral? They just loosen the earth and you sink down by yourself.

"Take the wheel, Harry!" said the nervous lady driver. "There's a tree coming straight for us!"

"I hate paying my income tax."
"You should be a good citizen – why don't you pay with a smile?"
"I'd like to but they insist on money...!"

Mr Jones met a neighbor carrying a front door.
"Why are you carrying that, Tom?" asked Mr Jones.
"I've lost my key," replied Tom.
"Oh," said Mr Jones, "so how will you get in?"
"It's all right – I've left the window open."

"The acoustics in this hall are marvelous, aren't they?"
"Pardon?"

"I don't think much of that new doctor."
"Why not?"
"Old Charlie Evans went to see him the other week.
He tapped Charlie's knee with that little hammer and
his leg fell off!"

"The trouble is," said the entertainer to the psychiatrist,
"that I can't sing, I can't dance, I can't tell jokes, I can't
act, I can't play an instrument or juggle or do magic
tricks or do anything!"
"Then why don't you give up show business?"
"I can't – I'm a star!"

"Doctor! Doctor! I think I'm a dog!"
"Sit down, please."
"Oh no – I'm not allowed on the furniture."

A boy had the bad luck to break an arm playing
football. After his arm had been put in plaster, he
asked the doctor, "When you take the plaster off, will I
be able to play the violin?"
"Of course you will," said the doctor reassuringly.
"That's funny," said the boy. "I couldn't before you put it
on."

Mom: "Joe, time for your medicine."
Joe: "I'll put the bath on."
Mom: "Why?"
Joe: "Because on the bottle it says 'to be taken in water.' "

A doctor had been attending a rich old man for some time, but it became apparent that the old chap had not long to live. Accordingly, the doctor advised his wealthy patient to put his affairs in order.
"Oh yes, I've done that," said the old gentleman. "I've only got to make my will. And do you know what I'm going to do with all my money? I'm going to leave it to the doctor who saves my life..."

"Doctor, come quickly!"
"What's the matter?"
"We can't get into our house!"
"That's scarcely my concern, is it?"
"Yes it is. The baby's swallowed the front door key!"

"Doctor Sawbones speaking."
"Oh, doctor, my wife's just dislocated her jaw. Can you come over in, say, three or four weeks time?"

"This is a most unusual complaint, Mrs Quilch. Have you had it before?"
"Yes, doctor."
"Well, you've got it again."

A man rushed into the doctor's surgery, jumped on the doctor's back, and started screaming "One! Two! Three! Four!"

"Wait a minute!" yelled the doctor, struggling to free himself. "What do you think you're doing?"

"Well, doctor," said the eccentric man, "they did say I could count on you!"

"Doctor! Doctor! My sister thinks she's a lift."

"Tell her to come in."

"I can't. She doesn't stop at this floor."

Doctor: "Say one-hundred-and-one."

Patient: "Not ninety-nine?"

Doctor: "Well, everything's going up."

Doctor: "How is your husband's lumbago?"

Wife: "Not too good. I rubbed his neck with whiskey like you told me to and he broke his neck trying to lick it off!"

At a diplomatic reception, the Mexican general appeared in a magnificent uniform, liberally bespattered with medals and decorations.

"That's most impressive," said the US ambassador. "Tell me general, what did you get all those for?"

"In your money," replied the Mexican general, "About five dollars!"

Commissioned by a zoo to bring them some baboons, the big game hunter devised a novel scheme to trap them – his only requirements being a sack, a gun, and a particularly vicious and bad-tempered dog. He tramped into the jungle with his assistant, and after several weeks they finally reached an area where baboons were numerous – though that didn't make them any easier to catch.

"This is what we'll do," he explained to his baffled assistant. "I'll climb this tree and shake the branches; if there are any baboons up there, they will then fall to the ground – and the dogs will bite their tails and immobilize them so that you can pick them up quite safely and put them in the sack."

"But what do I need a gun for?" asked the assistant.

"If I should fall out of the tree by mistake, shoot the dog!"

A woman just back from the United States was telling her friends about the trip.

"When my husband first saw the Grand Canyon, his face dropped a mile," she said.

"Why, was he disappointed with the view?"

"No, he fell over the edge."

A policeman saw a man dressed as a cowboy in the street, complete with huge stetson hat, spurs, and six shooters.

"Excuse me, sir," said the policeman, "who are you?"

"My name's Tex, officer," said the cowboy.

"Tex, eh?" said the policeman, "Are you from Texas?"

"Nope, Louisiana."

"Louisiana? So why are you called Tex?"

"Don't want to be called Louise, do I?"

A new hotel porter in Paris was instructed by the manager that it was important to call the guests by their names in order to make them feel welcome and that the easiest way to find out their name was to look at their luggage. Armed with this advice, the porter took two guests up to their rooms, put down their bags, and said, "I hope you 'ave a very 'appy stay 'ere in Paris, Mr and Mrs Genuine Cow'ide."

"What do you think of this suit? I had it made in Hong Kong."

"Very nice, but what's that hump on the back?"

"Oh, that's the tailor. He's still working on it."

A huge American car screeched to a halt in a sleepy English village, and the driver called out to a local inhabitant, "Say, am I on the right road for Shakespeare's birthplace?"

"Ay, straight on zur," said the rustic, "but no need to hurry. He's dead."

"I hope this plane doesn't travel faster than sound," said the old lady to the stewardess.
"Why?"
"Because my friend and I want to talk, that's why."

Having asked for shelter for the night at an English monastery, the traveler was surprised and delighted to be given a magnificent supper of fish and chips.
"That was absolutely superb!" he enthused to the monk who had been serving him. "That piece of fish was wonderful, and beautifully cooked. And as for the chips – they were the tastiest I've ever had in my life. Well done Brother."
"Oh you must thank Brother Ambrose for those," came the reply. "I'm the fish friar – he's the chip monk..."

A man sat on a train chewing gum and staring vacantly into space, when suddenly an old woman sitting opposite said, "It's no good you talking to me, young man, I'm stone deaf!"

"When we got to Benidorm the hotel was so full I had to sleep on a door across two tables."
"Was it comfortable?"
"Oh yes, but a bit draughty around the mailbox."

"Last time my wife and I traveled on the ferry from Newhaven to Dieppe, we had six meals."
"Six meals for that short crossing?"
"Three down and three up."

"I went fly-fishing yesterday."
"Catch anything?"
"Yes, a three-pound bluebottle."

"How should I have played that last shot?" the bad golfer asked his partner.
"Under an assumed name."

"My dog plays chess."
"Your dog plays chess? He must be really clever!"
"Oh, I don't know. I usually beat him three times out of four."

The big game-hunter was showing his friends his hunting trophies. Drawing their attention to a lion skin rug on the floor he said, "I shot this fellow in Africa. Didn't want to kill such a magnificent beast, of course, but it was either him or me."
"Well," said a guest, "he certainly makes a better rug than you would!"

"May I go swimming, Mommy?"
"No, you may not. There are sharks here."
"But Daddy's swimming."
"He's insured."

Did you hear about the boxing referee who used to work at a space rocket launching site? If a fighter was knocked down he'd count "Ten, nine, eight, seven..."

"My brother's a professional boxer."
"Heavyweight?"
"No, featherweight. He tickles his opponents to death."

"How do you spell wrong?"
"R-o-n-g."
"That's wrong."
"That's what you asked for, isn't it?"

One unfortunate teacher started off a lesson with the following instruction, "I want you all to give me a list of the lower animals, starting with Georgina Clark..."

Music master: "Brian, if 'f' means forte, what does 'ff' mean?"
Brian: "Eighty!"

Teacher: "You seem to be exceedingly ignorant, Williams – have you read Dickens?"
Williams: "No Sir."
Teacher: "Have you read Shakespeare?"
Williams: "No Sir."
Teacher: "Well, what have you read?"
Williams: "Er...er...I've red hair, Sir."

Teacher: "Mason, what is the outer part of a tree called?"
Mason: "Don't know, Sir."
Teacher: "Bark, boy, bark!"
Mason: "Woof-woof!"

Miss: "Why do we put a hyphen in a bird-cage?"
Stella: "For a parrot to perch on, Miss."

"Sir!" said Alexander. "Empty Coke tins, fish-and-chip papers, plastic bags, used tissues, broken bottles, empty boxes..."
"Alexander!" snapped the teacher. "You're talking rubbish again!"

"Frank," said the weary math teacher, "if you had seven dollars in your pocket, and seven dollars in another pocket, what would you have?"
"Someone else's trousers on!"

"Anne, can you spell 'banana' for me?"
"Well, sir, I know how to start, but I don't know when to stop!"

"How old would you say I am, Francis?" the teacher asked.
"Forty, sir," said the boy promptly.
"You seem very sure," said the puzzled teacher. "What makes you think I'm 40?"
"My big brother's 20, sir," replied the boy, "and you're twice as daft as he is!"

"Melanie," said the teacher sharply, "you've been doing Rebecca's homework for her again! I recognized your writing in her exercise book."
"I haven't, Miss," declared Melanie. "It's just that we use the same pencil!"

"Philip," asked the chemistry teacher, "what is HNO 3?"
"Oh, er...just a minute, Miss, er...it's on the tip of my tongue..."
"Well in that case – spit it out. It's nitric acid!"

The primary class had been told to draw a scene representing the flight into Egypt.
One little tot proudly displayed a drawing of a Jumbo Jet containing the three members of the Holy Family – but also a fourth figure.
"When I said 'flight,' I didn't quite mean a jet plane," said the teacher. "However, we'll let that pass for now. But who is the fourth person on the plane?"
To which the little one replied, "That's Pontius Pilot!"

Damien was being severely ticked off by his father for fighting.

"Now, Damien," said his angry parent, "this will not do! You must learn that you can't have everything you want in this life. There must always be give and take."

"But there was, Dad!" protested the aggressive youngster. "I gave him a black eye and took the apple!"

"Eat up all your spinach, Jemima. It'll put color in your cheeks."

"But who wants to have green cheeks?"

"Dad, there's a man at the door collecting for the new swimming pool."

"Give him a glass of water!"

Susannah was watching her big sister covering her face with cream. "What's that for?" she asked.

"To make me beautiful," came the reply.

Susannah then watched in silence as she wiped her face clean. "Doesn't work, does it?" was the moppet's comment.

"My boyfriend says I look like a dishy Italian!" said Miss Conceited.

"He's right," said her brother.

"Sophia Loren?"

"No – spaghetti!"

"Is my dinner hot?" asked the excessively late husband.

"It should be," said his furious wife, "it's been on the fire since seven o'clock!"

"Mom, can I have 10 cents for being good?"

"All right, but I wish you could be good-for-nothing!"

Little Jackie's mother was on the telephone to the boy's dentist.

"I don't understand it," she complained, "I thought his treatment would only cost me $10, but you've charged me $40."

"It is usually $10, madam," agreed the dentist, "but Jackie yelled so loudly that three of my other patients ran away!"

Alfie had been listening to his sister practice her singing. "Sis," he said, "I wish you'd sing Christmas carols."

"That's nice of you Alfie," she said, "why?"

"Then I'd only have to hear you once a year!"

"I don't think my Mom knows much about children."

"Why do you say that?"

"Because she always puts me to bed when I'm wide awake, and gets me up when I'm sleepy!"

"How old is your Grandad?"
"I dunno, but we've had him a long time."

When Mr Maxwell's wife left him, he couldn't sleep.
She had taken the bed.

The housewife answered a knock on the door and
found a total stranger standing on the doorstep.
"Excuse me for disturbing you, madam," he said
politely, "but I pass your house every morning on my
way to work, and I've noticed that every day you
appear to be hitting your son on the head with a loaf of
bread."
"That's right."
"Every day you hit him on the head with a loaf of
bread, and yet this morning you were clouting him with
a chocolate gateau...?"
"Well, today's his birthday."

"Stephen, it's time for your violin lesson."
"Oh, fiddle!"

Little brother: "Look sis, I've got a pack of cards."
Big sister: "Big deal!"

"Steve, you've been fighting again, haven't you?"

"Yes, Mom."

"You must try to control your temper. Didn't I tell you to count to ten?"

"Yes, but Vic's Mom only told him to count up to five, so he hit me first!"

Sandra and Simon were arguing furiously over the breakfast table.

"Oh, you're stupid!" shouted Simon.

"Simon!" said their father, "that's quite enough of that! Now say you're sorry."

"All right," said Simon. "Sandra, I'm sorry you're stupid."

Why was the Egyptian girl worried?

'Cos her Daddy was a Mummy.

What has webbed feet and fangs?

Count Quackula.

Why is Dracula so unpopular?
'Cos he's a pain in the neck.

Who said "Shiver me timbers!" on the ghost ship?
The skeleton crew.

Why is a turkey like an evil little creature?
'Cos it's always a-gobblin'...

Why did the skeleton go the party?
For a rattling good time!

"Bring me a crocodile sandwich immediately."
"I'll make it snappy, sir."

What's wrong with this fish?
Long time, no sea.

"There's a fly in my soup!"
"The little rascals don't care what they eat, do they?"

The psychiatrist was surprised to see a tortoise come into his office. "What can I do for you, Mr Tortoise?" asked the psychiatrist.
"I'm terribly shy, doctor," said the tortoise, "I want you to cure me of that."
"No problem. I'll soon have you out of your shell."

Why was the young kangaroo thrown out by his mother?
For smoking in bed.

A large sailing ship was at anchor off the coast of Mauritius, and two dodos watched the sailors rowing ashore.
"We'd better hide," said the first dodo.
"Why?" asked the second.
"Because," said the first, "we're supposed to be extinct, silly!"

"My budgie lays square eggs."
"That's amazing! Can it talk as well?"
"Yes, but only one word."
"What's that?"
"Ouch!"

The swing doors of the Wild West saloon crashed open and in came Little Pete, black with fury. "All right!" he raged, "all right! Who did it? What goddam varmint painted my horse blue?"
And the huge figure of Black Jake, notorious gunfighter and town baddie, rose from a chair by the door. "It was me, shrimp," he drawled, bunching his gigantic fists, "what about it?"
"Oh, well, er," stammered Little Pete wretchedly, "all I wanted to say was...er...when are you going to give it another coat?"

Two flies were on a cornflakes packet. "Why are we running so fast?" asked one.
"Because," said the second, "it says 'tear along the dotted line'!"

A family of tortoises went into a cafe for some ice-cream. They sat down and were about to start when Father Tortoise said, "I think it's going to rain. Junior, will you pop home and fetch my umbrella?"
So off went Junior Tortoise for his father's umbrella, but three days later he still hadn't returned.
"I think, dear," said Mother Tortoise to Father Tortoise, "we'd better eat Junior's ice-cream before it melts."
And a voice from the door said, "If you do that, I won't go!"

A man buying a camel was advised that to make it walk he should say "Few!"; to make it run he should say "Many!"; and to make it stop he should say "Amen!" At his first ride all went well. "Few!" he called, and off the camel went. "Many!" he shouted, and the camel began to run – straight for the edge of a cliff.
But the new owner had forgotten the word to make the camel stop! As the cliff edge came closer he called out in terror, "Lord save me! Lord save me! Amen!" And of course the camel stopped – right on the edge of the precipice. Whereupon the rider mopped his brow in relief and said, "Phew, that was clo-AAAAGH!"

Two fish were swimming in a stream when it began to rain. "Quick," said one fish to the other, "Let's swim under that bridge, otherwise we'll get wet!"

"Who's been eating my porridge?" squeaked Baby Bear.
"Who's been eating my porridge?" cried Mother Bear.
"Burp!" said Father Bear.

What happened at the badly organized milking contest? There was udder chaos.

Why are skunks always arguing?
'Cos they like to raise a stink.

If 20 dogs run after one dog, what time is it?
Twenty after one.

"We had roast boar for dinner last night."
"Was it a wild boar?"
"Well, it wasn't very pleased."

A man standing at a bus-stop was eating fish and chips.
Next to him stood a lady with her little dog, which
became very excited at the smell of the man's supper
and began whining and jumping up at him. "Do you
mind if I throw him a bit?" said the man to the lady.
"Not at all," she replied. Whereupon the man picked the
dog up and threw him over a wall...

"You have to be a good singer in our house, you know."
"Why's that?"
"There's no lock on the bathroom door."

"I'd like to buy a dog."

"Certainly, sir. Any particular breed? A Red Setter, perhaps?"

"No, not a red setter."

"A Golden Labrador?"

"No, not a Golden Labrador. I don't want a colored dog, just a black and white one."

"Why a black and white one, sir?"

"Isn't the license cheaper?"

Good news! At school today there will be free Coca-Cola for everyone... the bad news is that straws are 50 cents each!

A child one Christmas time asked for some paper and crayons in order to draw a crib. Eventually the artistic masterpiece was displayed for parental approval. The manger, the shepherds, Jesus, and the Holy Family were duly admired. "But what's that in the corner?" asked Mother.

"Oh, that's their TV," replied the child.

"What did you learn in school today, son?"

"I learned that those sums you did for me were wrong!"

"Rebecca, you've been a long time putting salt in the salt-cellar."

"Well, Mom, you can't get much at a time through that little hole in the top."

"Do you look in the mirror after you've washed?"
"No, I look in the towel!"

Grandma: "You've left all your crusts, Mary. When I
was your age I ate every one."
Mary: "Do you still like crusts, Grandma?"
Grandma: "Yes, I do."
Mary: "Well, you can have mine."

Pa was taking Danny around the museum when they
came across a magnificent stuffed lion in a glass case.
"Pa," asked the puzzled Danny, "how did they shoot
the lion without breaking the glass?"

"Mom, Mom! Dad's fallen over the cliff!"
"My goodness! Is he hurt?"
"I dunno – he hadn't stopped falling when I left!"

Midge was scribbling industriously over some paper
with a pencil when her mother asked her what she
was drawing.
"I'm not drawing, Mom," she said indignantly, "I'm
writing a letter to Jenny."
"But you can't write," Mom pointed out.
"That's all right," said Midge, "Jenny can't read."

"Dad, would you like to save some money?"
"I certainly would, son. Any suggestions?"
"Sure. Why not buy me a bike, then I won't wear my shoes out so fast."

"Who broke the window?"
"It was Andrew, Dad. He ducked when I threw a stone at him."

"Mom, do you think the baby would like some blotting paper to eat?
"No, dear, I don't think he would. Why?"
"He's just swallowed a bottle of ink..."

"Vicar told us that in the Bible it says we're made of dust."
"That's right."
"So when I go swimming, why don't I get muddy?"

Jimmy was caught by his mother in the pantry. "And what do you think you're up to?" she asked furiously.
"I'm up to my seventh jelly tart," said Jimmy.

"Mom, will you wash my face?"

"Why can't you wash it yourself?"

" 'Cos that'll mean my hands getting wet, and they don't need washing!"

"So you are distantly related to the family next door, are you?"

"Yes – their dog is our dog's brother."

A rather stern aunt had been staying with Sharon's parents, and one day she said to the little girl, "Well, Sharon, I'm going tomorrow. Are you sorry?"

"Oh yes, Auntie," replied Sharon. "I thought you were going today."

"No, Billy, you can't play with the hammer. You'll hurt your fingers."

"No I won't, Dad. Sis is going to hold the nails for me."

A scoutmaster asked one of his troop what good deed he had done for the day. "Well, Skip," said the scout. "Mom had only one dose of castor oil left, so I let my baby brother have it."

"Come here, you greedy wretch. I'll teach you to eat all your sister's birthday chocs."
"It's all right, Dad, I know how."

"I had a funny dream last night, Mom."
"Did you?"
"I dreamed I was awake, but when I woke up I found I was asleep."

"Mossop! Why are you late this morning?"
"I got married, sir."
"Very well, but see that it doesn't happen again."

"Very well, my boy," said the manager, "I'll take you on. I take it you're not afraid of early hours?"
"Oh no, sir," said the teenage applicant, "you can't close too early for me!"

"Why did you leave your last job?"
"Something the boss said."
"Was he abusive?"
"Not exactly."
"What did he say, then?"
"You're fired!"

"I was a waiter at the Hotel Splendiferous for three months, but I had to leave on account of the head waiter's nerves."

"His nerves?"

"He couldn't stand the sound of breaking crockery."

An apprentice blacksmith was told by his master to make a hammer. The lad had not the slightest idea how to begin, so he thought he'd be crafty and nip out and buy one. He duly showed the new hammer to his master who said, "That's excellent, boy! Now make 50 more just like it!"

"You play fair with me and I'll play fair with you," said the boss to the new worker. "Just remember : you can't do too much for a good employer."

"Don't worry, I won't."

"I just want you to remember one thing, Boyce," said the managing director to the new sales manager. "If at first you don't succeed – you're fired!"

"Come on, slowcoach," said the foreman to a tardy workman, "the hooter's gone."

"Don't look at me, guv. I didn't take it!"

325

"You're asking a lot of money for an unskilled man," said the foreman to a Cockney English job applicant, "and you've no experience of our kind of work at all, have you?"

"No, well," explained the hopeful one, "I fink I oughter have more money, 'cos it's so much 'arder when you don't know nuffink abaht it, ain't it?"

The butcher's boy had been dismissed for insolence, and vowed vengeance on his ex-employer. The following Saturday morning, when the shop was packed with people buying their weekend joints, he marched in, elbowed his way to the counter and slapped down one very, very dead cat.
"There you are, guv!" he called out cheerily, "that makes up the dozen you ordered!"

"I need a smart boy," said the boss to the young applicant. "Someone quick to take notice."
"Oh, I can do that, sir. I had it twice last week."

The manager of a shop observed one of his customers in a furious argument with a junior assistant. As he hurried over, the customer finally yelled, "...and I shall never come into this place again!" And he stalked out, slamming the door behind him. "Hicks," said the manager severely, "how many more times must I tell you that the customer is always right?"
"As you wish, sir," said the junior. "He was saying you were a lop-eared, bald-headed, brainless twit!"

The apprentice electrician was on his first job. "Take hold of those two wires, Alex," said his master, "and rub them together."
Alex did as he was bid, and his master said, "Do you feel anything?"
"No," said Alex.
"That's good – so don't touch those other two wires or you'll get a nasty shock!"

The young lad had applied for a job, and was asked his full name.
"Aloysius Montmorency Geoghan," he replied.
"How do you spell that?" asked the manager.
"Er – sir – er – can't you just put it down without spelling it?"

"Did your previous employer give you a reference?"
"Yes, but I left it at home."
"What does it say?"
"Er, well, it says I was one of the best employers that he had ever turned out..."

"If you're going to work here, young man," said the boss, "one thing you must learn is that we are very keen on cleanliness in this firm. Did you wipe your feet on the mat as you came in?"
"Oh, yes sir."
"And another thing, we are very keen on truthfulness. There is no mat."

"Why did you leave your last employment?"
"The boss accused me of stealing a five dollar note."
"But why didn't you make him prove it?"
"He did."

A diner in a restaurant was handed the menu by the waiter who, the diner was disconcerted to observe, stood by the table scratching his bottom.

"I say, waiter," said the diner icily, "have you got an itchy bottom?"

"No, sir," replied the waiter. "Only what's on the menu!"

Did you hear about the really high-powered business tycoon? He had a tall secretary for taking dictation in longhand, a small secretary for taking dictation in shorthand, and a tiny secretary for taking footnotes!

"Don't you like being a telegraph linesman?"

"No, it's driving me up the pole."

"I thought, Jessop, that you wanted yesterday afternoon off because you were seeing your dentist?"

"That's right, sir."

"So how come I saw you coming out of the football ground at the end of a game with a friend?"

"That was my dentist."

"This loaf is nice and warm!"

"It should be – the cat's been sitting on it all day!"

"Mr Butcher, have you got a sheep's head?"
"No, madam, it's just the way I part my hair."

Why did the lazy man get a job in a bakery?
'Cos he wanted a good loaf.

"I want a hair-cut, please."
"Certainly, sir. Which one?"

A worker on a building site rushed up to the foreman.
"Gaffer! Gaffer!" he cried. "Someone's just dropped a trowel from the top of the scaffolding and sliced my ear off!"
Immediately, the foreman organized a search party to find the ear in the hope that surgeons might be able to sew it on again.
"Here it is!" cried one of the searchers, waving an ear.
"No, that's not it," said the injured workman. "Mine had a pencil behind it!"

"I'm the boss and you're nothing! What are you?"
"Nothing."
"And what am I?"
"Boss over nothing."
"Pshaw! You're next to an idiot."
"Very well, I'll move."

What did the spider say to the beetle?
"Stop bugging me."

What did the tie say to the hat?
"You go on ahead and I'll hang around."

What did the picture say to the wall?
"I've got you covered."

What is the best thing to take into the desert?
A thirst-aid kit.

Who was the first underwater spy?
James Pond.

How do you milk a mouse?
You can't – the bucket won't fit under it.

What is hairy and coughs?
A coconut with a cold.

What do you call a foreign body in a chip pan?
An Unidentified Frying Object.

When is it bad luck to be followed by a black cat?
When you're a mouse.

What cake wanted to rule the world?
Attila the Bun.

Where does a general keep his armies?
Up his sleevies.

How did Noah see the animals in the Ark?
By flood-lighting.

What swings through trees and is very dangerous?
A chimpanzee with a machine gun.

What has four legs, whiskers, a tail, and flies?
A dead cat.

What do cannibals eat for breakfast?
Buttered host.

What lies at the bottom of the sea and shivers?
A nervous wreck.

Why did the man take a pencil to bed?
To draw the curtains...I'd tell you another joke about a
pencil, but it hasn't any point.

Why did the burglar take a shower?
He wanted to make a clean getaway.

Why do idiots eat biscuits?
Because they're crackers.

What do you call an American drawing?
Yankee Doodle.

Why do bears wear fur coats?
They'd look silly in plastic macs.

What is cowhide most used for?
Holding cows together.

What training do you need to be a rubbish collector?
None, you pick it up as you go along.

"I was once in a play called *Breakfast In Bed*."
"Did you have a big role?"
"No, just toast and marmalade."

The effect of TV commercials on young viewers can be gauged from this version of part of the Lord's Prayer, as rendered by a small boy: "Give us this day our oven-fresh, slow-baked, vitamin-enriched, protein-packed, nourishing, delicious, wholemeal daily bread!"

"What sort of an act do you do?"
"I bend over backwards and pick up a handkerchief with my teeth."
"Anything else?"
"Then I bend over backwards and pick up my teeth."

School meals are not generally popular with those that have to eat them, and sometimes with good reason.
"What kind of pie do you call this?" asked one schoolboy indignantly.
"What's it taste of?" asked the cook.
"Glue!"
"Then it's apple pie – the plum pie tastes of soap."

"Alfred, if I had 20 marbles in my right trousers pocket, 20 marbles in my left trousers pocket, 40 marbles in my right hip pocket and 40 marbles in my left hip pocket – what would I have?"
"Heavy trousers, sir!"

"Any complaints?" asked the teacher during school dinner.

"Yes, sir," said one bold lad, "these peas are awfully hard, sir."

The master dipped a spoon into the peas on the boy's plate and tasted them. "They seem soft enough to me," he declared.

"Yes, they are now," agreed the boy, "I've been chewing them for the last half hour!"

Teacher: "What is the plural of mouse?"
Infant: "Mice."
Teacher: "And what is the plural of baby?"
Infant: "Twins."

Teacher: "Now, Harrison, if your father borrows $10 from me and pays me back at $1 a month, at the end of 6 months how much will he owe me?"
Harrison: "$10, sir."
Teacher: "I'm afraid you don't know much about arithmetic, Harrison."
Harrison: "I'm afraid you don't know much about my father, sir."

Teacher: "Martin, I've taught you everything I know, and you're still ignorant!"

Teacher: "Tommy Russell, you're late again."
Tommy: "Sorry, sir. It's my bus – it's always coming late."
Teacher: "Well, if it's late again tomorrow, catch an earlier one."

Teacher: "Alan, give me a sentence starting with 'I.'"
Alan: "I is-"
Teacher: "No, Alan. You must always say 'I am.'"
Alan: "Oh right. 'I am the ninth letter of the alphabet.'"

Teacher: "Ford, you're late for school again. What is it this time?"
Ford: "I sprained my ankle, sir."
Teacher: "That's a lame excuse."

Teacher: "Spell the word 'needle,' Kenneth."
Kenneth: "N-e-i-"
Teacher: "No, Kenneth, there's no 'i' in needle."
Kenneth: "Then it's a rotten needle, Miss!"

Teacher: "Carol, what is 'can't' short for?"
Carol: "Cannot."
Teacher: "And what is 'don't' short for?"
Carol: "Doughnut!"

Teacher: "Matthew, what is the climate of New Zealand?"
Matthew: "Very cold, sir."
Teacher: "Wrong."
Matthew: "But sir! When they send us meat, it always arrives frozen!"

Teacher: "Anyone here quick at picking up music?"
Terence and Tony: "I am, sir!"
Teacher: "Right, you two. Move that piano!"

The agitated woman had rung 999.
"Police, fire or ambulance?" asked the operator.
"I want a vet!" demanded the panic-stricken woman.
"A vet?" said the emergency service operator in surprise. "What for?"
"To open my bulldog's jaws."
"But why did you ring 999?"
"There's a burglar in them."

The constable was calling up his station on his pocket radio. "I'm outside the Plaza Cinema in the High Street," he reported. "A man has been robbed – I've got one of them."
"Which one?"
"The one that was robbed."

338

"What is your occupation?" asked the magistrate.

"I'm a locksmith, your honor."

"And what were you doing in the jeweler's shop at three in the morning when the police officers entered?"

"Making a bolt for the door!"

A policeman was escorting a prisoner to jail when his hat blew off.

"Shall I run and get it for you?" asked the prisoner obligingly.

"You must think I'm daft," said the policeman. "You stand here and I'll get it."

"What makes you think the prisoner was drunk?" asked the magistrate.

"Well, your honor," replied the arresting officer, "I saw him lift up a manhole cover and walk away with it, and when I asked him what it was for he said 'I want to listen to it on my record-player'!"

"It's a pity you've gone on hunger strike," said the convict's wife on visiting day.

"Why?"

"I've put a file in your cake."

Policeman: "Why are you driving with a bucket of water on the passenger seat?"

Motorist: "So I can dip my headlights."

Three men were in the dock, and the judge, who had a terrible squint, said to the first, "How do you plead?"

"Not guilty," said the second.

"I'm not talking to you," snapped the judge.

"I didn't say a word," said the third.

The criminal mastermind found one of his gang sawing the legs off his bed. "What are you doing that for?" demanded the crook boss.

"Only doing what you ordered," said the stupid thug. "You told me to lie low for a bit!"

"Now as I understand it, sir" said the policeman to the motorist, "you were driving this vehicle when the accident occurred. Can you tell me what happened?"

"I'm afraid not, constable," replied the motorist. "I had my eyes shut!"

A jeweler standing behind the counter of his shop was astounded to see a man come hurtling head-first through the window.

"What on earth are you up to?" he demanded.

"I'm terribly sorry," said the man, "I forgot to let go of the brick!"

Two petty crooks had been sent by the Big Boss to steal a van-load of goods from a bathroom suppliers. One stayed in the van as look-out and the other went into the storeroom. Fifteen minutes went by, then half an hour, then an hour – and no sign of him. The look-out crook finally grew impatient and went to look for his partner in crime. Inside the store the two came face to face. "Where have you been?" demanded the worried look-out.

"The boss told me to take a bath, but I can't find the soap and towel!"

"I'll have to report you, sir" said the traffic cop to the speeding driver. "You were doing 85 miles an hour."
"Nonsense, officer," declared the driver. "I've only been in the car for ten minutes!"

How does an elephant go up a tree?
It stands on an acorn and waits for it to grow.

"Would you like to play with our new dog?"
"He looks very fierce. Does he bite?"
"That's what I want to find out."

"What's your new dog's name?"
"Dunno – he won't tell me."

WENDY

A man went into a pet shop to buy a parrot. He was shown an especially fine one which he liked the look of, but he was puzzled by the two strings which were tied to its feet.

"What are they for?" he asked the pet shop manager.

"Ah well, sir," came the reply, "that's a very unusual feature of this particular parrot. You see, he's a trained parrot, sir – he used to be in a circus. If you pull the string on his left foot he says 'Hello!' and if you pull the string on his right foot he says 'Goodbye!' "

"And what happens if I pull both the strings at the same time?"

"I fall off my perch, you fool!" screeched the parrot.

"Have you ever seen a man-eating tiger?"

"No, but in the cafe next door I once saw a man eating chicken!"

A mean horseman went into a saddler's shop and asked for one spur. "One spur?" asked the saddler. "Surely you mean a pair of spurs, sir?"

"No, just one," replied the horseman, "If I can get one side of the horse to go, the other side is bound to come with it!"

First cat: "How did you get on in the milk-drinking contest?"

Second cat: "Oh, I won by six laps!"

The owner of a donkey-cart called the vet to a country lane. "What's the matter?" asked the vet.

"I don't know," was the reply, "he just won't move."

"I'll soon fix that," said the vet. "I'll give him some of my special medicine."

About three seconds after the donkey had taken the medicine he went galloping off up the lane with his cart rattling behind him.

"Fantastic!" exclaimed his owner. "What do I owe you?"

"That'll be 50 cents, please," said the vet.

"Well, you'd better give me $1's worth or I'll never catch him!"

Why does an ostrich have such a long neck?
Because its head is so far from its body.

A farmer was showing a schoolboy round his farm when they came to a field where the farmer's sheep were grazing.

"How many sheep do you reckon there are?" the farmer asked proudly.

"Seven hundred and sixty-four" replied the boy after a few seconds.

The farmer gaped. "That's exactly right, boy. How did you count them so quickly?"

"Simple," said the boy genius. "I just counted the legs and divided by four!"

A Dubliner was in court charged with parking his car in a restricted area. The judge asked if he had anything to say in his defence. "They shouldn't put up such misleading notices," said the Dubliner.

"It said FINE FOR PARKING HERE."

Paddy and Mick were sent to jail in a high security prison, but they developed an ingenious method of communicating with each other by means of a secret code and banging on the pipes. However, their scheme broke down when they were transferred to different cells.

NEWSFLASH!
Thieves escaped with over half a million pounds from a Galway bank last night. Police are baffled trying to figure out the motive for the crime.

When Stinker's Gran took him to a big department store she lost him, and then found him gazing down at the escalator.
"Are you all right?" she asked.
"Sure," replied Stinker. "I'm just waiting for my chewing-gum to come round again."

Did you hear about the granny who plugged her electric blanket into the toaster by mistake? She spent the night popping out of bed.

One Irishman was showing off his knowledge to another, so he asked him if he knew what shape the world was.

"I don't," said the second.

"It's the same shape as the buttons on my jacket," said the first.

"Square," said the second.

"That's my Sunday jacket," said the first. "I meant my weekday jacket. Now what shape is the world?"

"Square on Sundays, round on weekdays," said the second Irishman.

It was the Irish chess championships and the two Irish grandmasters were sitting with their heads bent over the board, contemplating their strategies. Radio, TV and the newspapers waited with bated breath for the next move. Hours went by and there was no sign of anything happening. Then one of the grandmasters looked up and said, "Oh. Is it my move?"

First Irishman: "What's Mick's other name?"
Second Irishman: "Mick who?"

"Anyone who isn't confused here doesn't really understand what's going on."

A salesman was trying to persuade a housewife to buy a life assurance policy. "Just imagine, if your husband were to die," he said. "What would you get?"

"Oh, a sheepdog, I think," replied the wife. "They're so well-behaved."

John kept pestering his parents to buy a video, but they said they couldn't afford one. So one day John came home clutching a package containing a brand-new video. "Wherever did you get the money to pay for that?" asked his father suspiciously.

"It's all right, Dad," replied John, "I traded the TV in for it."

Jane: "Have you noticed that your mother smells a bit funny these days?"
Wayne: "No. Why?"
Jane: "Well your sister told me she was giving her a bottle of toilet water for her birthday."

Andy was late for school. "Andy!" roared his mother. "Have you got your socks on yet?"
"Yes, Mom," replied Andy. "All except one."

Stinker and Freddie were discussing their dads.
"Mine's a bit of a magician," said Stinker.
"How do you mean?" asked Freddie.
"Once he starts waving his magic slipper around, I disappear."

"Millicent! What did I say I'd do if I found you with your fingers in the butter again?"
"That's funny, Mom. I can't remember either."

Doctor: "Now tell me, Granny Perkins, how you happened to burn both your ears."

Granny Perkins: "I was doing the ironing when the telephone rang, and I picked up the iron and put that to my ear by mistake."

Doctor: "But you burnt both your ears!"

Granny Perkins: "Yes, well as soon as I'd put the phone down it rang again!"

Young Jimmy was having tea with his Gran.

"Would you like a biscuit?" she asked.

"Yes, please," replied Jimmy.

"What good manners you have," said his Gran. "I do like to hear young people say 'please' and 'thank you.' "

"I'll say them both if I can have a big slice of that cake," replied Jimmy.

Doctor: "You seem to be in excellent health, Mrs Brown. Your pulse is as steady and regular as clockwork."

Mrs Brown: "That's because you've got your hand on my watch."

Happily innocent of all golfing lore, Sam watched with interest the efforts of the man in the bunker to play his ball. At last it rose amid a cloud of sand, hovered in the air, and then dropped on the green and rolled into the hole.

"Oh my," Sam chuckled, "he'll have a tough time getting out of that one!"

"My wife says that if I don't give up golf she'll leave me."

"Say, that's tough, old man."

"Yeah, I'm going to miss her."

"Can ye see your way to letting me have a golf ball, Jock?" Ian asked his old friend.

"But Ian, you said you were going to stop playing golf," said Jock, reluctantly handing over an old spare.

"By degrees, Jock. By degrees," replied Ian pocketing the ball. "I've stopped buying balls as a first step."

Where is Dracula's office in America?
In the Vampire State Building.

What were the Chicago gangster's last words?
"Who put that violin in my violin case?"

What do you call an American with a lavatory on his head?
John.

Knock, knock.
Who's there?
Sonia.
Sonia who?
Sonia shoe. I can smell it from here.

"Let me inform you, young man," said the slow elderly golfer, "I was playing this game before you were born." "That's all very well, but I'd be obliged if you'd try to finish it before I die."

A man who bought a dog took it back, complaining that it made a mess all over the house. "I thought you said it was house-trained," he moaned.
"So it is," said the previous owner. "It won't go anywhere else."

A motorist ran into a shop.
"Do you own a black and white cat?" he asked. "No," replied the shopkeeper.
"Oh dear," said the motorist, "I must have run over a nun."

Mandy had a puppy on a lead. She met Sandy and said, "I just got this puppy for my little brother."
"Really?" said Sandy. "Whoever did you find to make a swap like that?"

Darren came home with two black eyes and a face covered in blood. His mother was horrified. "You've been fighting," she said. "Who did this to you?"
"I don't know his name," replied Darren. "But I'd know him if I met him again. I've got half his left ear in my pocket."

Did you hear about the sword swallower who swallowed an umbrella?
He wanted to put something away for a rainy day.

Cannibal to his daughter: "Now you are nearly old enough to be married, we must start looking around for an edible bachelor."

Mrs Brown was always complaining about her husband. "If things go on like this I'll have to leave him," she moaned to Mrs Jenkins.
"Give him the soft-soap treatment," said Mrs Jenkins.
"I tried that," replied Mrs Brown, "it didn't work. He spotted it at the top of the stairs."

"Waiter, waiter, there's a fly in my soup!"
"Don't worry, sir, the spider in the butter will catch it."

A man coughed violently, and his false teeth shot across the room and smashed against the wall.

"Oh dear," he said, "whatever shall I do? I can't afford a new set."

"Don't worry," said his friend. "I'll get a pair from my brother for you." The next day the friend came back with the teeth, which fitted perfectly.

"This is wonderful," said the man. "Your brother must be a very good dentist."

"Oh, he's not a dentist," replied the friend, "he's an undertaker."

What did one virus say to another?
Stay away, I think I've got penicillin.

The village idiot sat on the side of the road with a fishing line down the drain. Feeling sorry for him, and wanting to humor him, a lady gave him 50 cents, and kindly asked "How many have you caught?"

"You're the tenth this morning," was the reply.

A small, thin, weedy little man went into a pub for a drink. He was fascinated by the barmaid, who was going bald, had droopy, bloodshot eyes, and was altogether extremely ugly. He turned to the man next to him and said, "What an amazing-looking barmaid." The man got hold of his coat collar and snarled, "That barmaid is my sister."

"Goodness," said the weedy little man. "Doesn't her face suit her!"

When the cow fell over the cliff, little Sarah couldn't stop laughing. After all, there was no point in crying over spilt milk.

What happens when plumbers die?
They go down the drain.

What's the name for a short-legged tramp?
A low-down bum.

A naughty child was irritating all the passengers on the flight from London to New York. At last one man could stand it no longer. "Hey kid," he shouted, "Why don't you go outside and play?"

How do you cure a headache?
Put your head through a window, and the pane will disappear.

Knock, knock.
Who's there?
Thumping.
Thumping who?
Thumping green and slimy just went up your trousers.

What do you get if you cross a cow with a mule?
Milk with a kick in it.

Mr Brown: "I hate to tell you, but your wife just fell in
the wishing well."
Mr Smith: "It works!"

Father: "How did the greenhouse get smashed?"
Arthur: "I was cleaning my catapult and it went off."

Why is it not safe to sleep on trains?
Because they run over sleepers.

Sharon: "I'm so homesick."
Sheila: "But this is your home!"
Sharon: "I know, and I'm sick of it!"

Did you hear about the woman who was so ugly she could make yogurt by staring at a pint of milk for an hour?

Sign on a chemist's shop: "We dispense with accuracy."

The transatlantic liner was experiencing particularly heavy weather, and Mrs Ramsbottom wasn't feeling well.
"Would you care for some more supper, madam?" asked the steward.
"No thanks," replied the wretched passenger. "Just throw it overboard to save me the trouble."

The scout troup had been on a long country ramble, and it was 6 p.m. before they arrived back at camp. Their leader did a roll-call and discovered that Cuthbert was missing. No one seemed to know where he was. The evening wore on, and the scout leader got more and more worried, until at 8 p.m., he saw young Cuthbert plodding up to his tent.

"Where have you been, Cuthbert?" he asked angrily. "We've all been worried about you."

"Well," said Cuthbert, "You must remember that field of cows we crossed before we forded the river?"

"Yes," replied the scout leader.

"Well," said Cuthbert, "as we were crossing it my beret flew off, and I had to try on 25 before I found the right one."

Mrs Brown: "Who was that at the door?"
Veronica: "A lady with a baby in a pram."
Mrs Brown: "Tell her to push off."

Sign in a cafe: "All drinking water in this establishment has been personally passed by the management."

Did you hear about the man who was so stupid that when he picked his nose he tore the lining of his hat?

Sign in a launderette: "Those using automatic washers should remove their clothes when the lights go out."

"Mommy, mommy, why do you keep poking daddy in the ribs?"
"If I don't, the fire will go out."

Why did the elephant cross the road?
To pick up the flattened chicken.

Two boys were watching TV when the fabulous face and figure of Bo Derek appeared on the screen.

"If I ever stop hating girls," said one to the other, "I think I'll stop hating her first."

Did you hear about the farmer's boy who hated the country?

He went to the big city and got a job as a shoe-shine boy, and so the farmer made hay while the son shone!

Sign in shop window:

FOR SALE Pedigree bulldog. House trained. Eats anything. Very fond of children.

"This morning my dad gave me soap flakes instead of corn flakes for breakfast!"

"I bet you were mad."

"Mad? I was foaming at the mouth!"

"Some girls think I'm handsome," said the young Romeo, "and some girls think I'm ugly. What do you think, Sheila?"

"A bit of both. Pretty ugly."

"You're ugly!"
"And you're drunk!"
"Yes, but in the morning I'll be sober!"

"Good news! I've been given a goldfish for my birthday...the bad news is that I don't get the bowl until my next birthday!"

Mr Grouch was enraged when young Joe from next door began throwing stones at his greenhouse.
"I'll teach you, you young imp of Satan!" roared the furious neighbor. "I'll teach you to throw stones at my greenhouse!"
"I wish you would," said the cheeky lad. "I've had three goes, and I haven't hit it yet!"

One very hot day an extremely small man went into a cafe, put his newspaper on a table and went to the counter. But on returning with a cup of tea he saw that his place had been taken by a huge, bearded, ferocious-looking man of some 300 pounds in weight, and six feet nine inches in height.
"Excuse me," said the little man to the big man, "but you're sitting in my seat."
"Oh yeah?" snarled the big man. "Prove it!"
"Certainly. You're sitting on my ice-cream."

Why did the golfer wear an extra pair of trousers?
In case he got a hole in one.

Postman: "Is this letter for you, sir? The name is all
smudged."
Man: "No, my name is Allsop."

"Why do you keep doing the backstroke?"
"I've just had lunch and don't want to swim on a full
stomach."

"Why are you covered in bruises?"
"I started to walk through a revolving door and then I
changed my mind."

"Is that Cohen, Cohen, Cohen & Cohen?"

"Yes, madam."

"May I speak to Mr Cohen, please? It's very important."

"I'm afraid Mr Cohen is on holiday."

"Oh... may I speak to Mr Cohen, then? It's extremely urgent."

"I'm afraid Mr Cohen is off sick."

"Oh dear... what about Mr Cohen? It's a matter of life and death."

"Mr Cohen is on business in Brussels."

"Oh Lord, I'm desperate! Can I speak to Mr Cohen, then?"

"Speaking."

How do you stop a cold going to your chest?
Tie a knot in your neck.

"What steps would you take," roared the sergeant-instructor, "if one of the enemy came at you with a bayonet?"
A small voice in the rear rank muttered, "Dirty great big ones!"

Two boys camping out in a back garden wanted to know the time, so they began singing at the top of their voices. Eventually a neighbor threw open his window and shouted down at them, "Hey! Less noise! Don't you know what the time is? It's three o'clock!"

"Tell me," said the hiker to the local yokel, "will this pathway take me to the main road?"
"No zur," replied the rustic, "you'll have to go by yourself!"

"No, no, no!" said the enraged businessman to the persistent salesman. "I cannot see you today!"
"That's fine," said the salesman, "I'm selling spectacles!"

Mr Timpson noticed his neighbor, Mr Simpson, searching very hard for something in his front garden.
"Have you lost something, Mr Simpson?" asked Mr Timpson.
"Yes," replied Mr Simpson. "I've mislaid my spectacles."
"Oh dear," said Mr Timpson, "Where did you last see them?"
"In my sitting-room," said Mr Simpson.
"In your sitting room?" queried Mr Timpson. "So why are you looking for them in your garden?"
"Oh," replied Mr Simpson, "there's more light out here!"

Charlie and Farley saw two men at a river bridge fishing in a most peculiar manner. One was holding the other over the parapet by his ankles and the second was hooking the fish out of the water with his hands! Strange though this angling technique may have been, it was remarkably successful, and the man being held over the bridge was throwing up big fish every few seconds. "Let's try that," Charlie said to Farley, and Farley agreed.
So on they walked until they came to another bridge, where Charley held onto Farley's ankles and waited for his friend to throw up lots of fish. But five minutes went by and Farley had caught nothing; ten minutes, twenty minutes – an hour, then two hours, and still no fish.
Then suddenly Farley called out,
"Charlie, pull me up quick! There's a train coming!"

"I don't think these photographs you've taken do me justice."
"You don't want justice – you want mercy!"

Two Irishmen looking for work saw a sign which read TREE FELLERS WANTED.
"Oh now, look at that," said Paddy. "What a pity there's only de two of us!"

Paddy went to a riding stable and hired a horse.
"Hold on for a moment," said the assistant as he helped him onto the horse, "aren't you putting that saddle on backwards?"
"You don't even know which way I want to go!"

There were two Irishmen painting a house.
Pat: "Have you got a good hold on that paint brush, Mick?"
Mick: "Yes, I have, Pat. Why?"
Pat: "Well, hold on tight, because I'm taking this ladder away."

You'll remember the Irishman who got a job as a doorman in a big building. He managed very well with the PUSH and PULL signs, but was seen struggling with his fingers under a door marked LIFT.

Paddy was telling Mick of his plans to make a lot of money. "I intend to buy a dozen swarms of bees and every morning at dawn I'm going to let them into the park opposite my house to spend all the day making honey, while I relax".
"But the park doesn't open until nine o'clock," protested Mick.
"I realize that", said Paddy, "but I know where there's a hole in the fence".

An Irishman joined the American Air Force and was making his first parachute jump. The instructor said, "When you jump out of the plane, shout 'Geronimo' and pull the rip-cord." When the Irishman woke up in hospital a few days later the first thing he said was "What was the name of that Indian again?"

The plane was circling at 5,000 meters and the Killarney Green Berets paratroop squad were about to make their first jump.
"Hold everything!" shouted the commanding officer.
"You're not wearing your parachute, O'Leary."
"It's all right, sir," replied O'Leary. "Sure, it's only a practice jump we're doing."

A tourist walked into a fish and chip shop in Derry.
"I'll have fish and chips twice," he ordered.
"Sure, I heard you the first time," came the reply.

Two Irishmen were out hunting when one of them saw a rabbit. "Quick," said the first, "shoot it."
"I can't," said the second, "my gun isn't loaded."
"Well," said the first, "you know that, and I know that, but the rabbit doesn't."

An American tourist traveling in Limerick came across a little antique shop in which he was lucky enough to pick up, for a mere $150, the skull of Brian Boru. Included in this price was a certificate of authenticity, signed by Brian Boru himself.
Ten years later, the tourist returned to Ireland and asked the antique shop owner if he had any more bargains.
"I've got the very thing for you," said the Irishman, "it's the genuine skull of Brian Boru."
"You swindler," said the American. "You sold me that ten years ago," and producing the skull, added, "Look, they're not even the same size."
"You have it all wrong," said the Irishman. "This is the skull of Brian Boru when he was a lad."

"Did you hear about the fool who keeps going round saying 'no'?"
"No."
"Oh, so it's you!"

A man is in a prison cell with no windows and no doors; there are no holes in the ceiling or trapdoors in the floor, yet in the morning the wardens find him gone.
How did he get out?
Through the doorway – there were no doors remember!

If a dog is tied to a rope 15 feet long, how can it reach a bone 30 feet away?
The rope isn't tied to anything!

When Dave Doyle was applying for a credit card, the manager of the credit card company asked him if he had much money in the bank.
"I have," said Dave.
"How much?" asked the manager.
"I don't know exactly," said Dave, "I haven't shaken it lately."

An Irishman went into a post office to see if there were any letters for him.
"I'll see, sir," said the clerk. "What is your name?"
"You're having me on now because I'm Irish," said the Irishman. "Won't you see the name on the envelope?"

Did you hear about the Irishman who spent an hour in a big store looking for a cap with a peak at the back?

Then there was the Irishman who was stranded for an hour when the elevator broke down.

Two Irishmen were walking down the street when one turned to the other and said, "Look, there's a dead pigeon."
"Where? Where?" said the second Irishman looking up at the sky.

Paddy and Mick were watching a John Wayne film on TV. In one scene John Wayne was riding madly toward a cliff.

"I bet you $10 he falls over that cliff," said Paddy.

"Done," said Mick. John Wayne rode straight over the cliff. As Mick handed over his $10, Paddy said, "I feel a bit guilty about this, I've seen the film before."

"So have I," said Mick, "but I didn't think he'd be fool enough to make the same mistake twice."

Pat and Mick were at a bingo session and one of them kept on looking over the other's shoulder and telling him when his numbers were being called.

Mick got annoyed and said, "Look, why don't you fill in your own card?"

"I can't," said Pat, "it's full."

Two Irishmen were out walking together when they saw a lorry pass by laden with grassy sods of earth for the laying of a lawn.

"Do you know, Mick," said one of them to the other, "if I ever get rich that's what I'll have done – send away my lawn to be cut."

Mick Murphy got a job as an assistant gardener at a big country house. One day he saw a bird bath for the first time.

"What's that for?" he asked the head gardener.

"That's a bird bath," he replied.

"I don't believe you," said Mick. "There isn't a bird in Creation who can tell the difference between Saturday night and any other night of the week."

Incidentally, did you hear about the Irish kidnapper?
He enclosed a stamped, self-addressed envelope with
the ransom note.

Two Irishmen, one very fat and the other very thin,
once decided to fight a duel with pistols. Their
seconds decided that the thin man had an unfair
advantage because of the bigger target that the fat
man presented. Finally they agreed that the figure of
the thin man could be chalked on the body of the fat
man and that any bullets hitting the fat man outside
the line would not count.

"What did Daddy say when he fell in the dung-heap?"
a farmer asked her son.
"Shall I leave out the swear words?"
"Yes."
"He didn't say anything."

A group of Chinamen who were on safari in Africa
came across a pride of lions. "Oh look," said one of
the lions. "A Chinese takeaway."

"When times were hard, a family of New York pigeons
moved to the top of the Empire State Building, and
every morning and every evening, the family left the
roost, flew around the top of the building and let their
droppings fall on to the street hundreds of feet below."
"I'm not sure I get the point of this story."
"Well, in hard times, you have to make a little go a
long way!"

What's the smelliest city in America?
Phew York.

First lion: "Every time I eat, I feel sick."
Second lion: "I know. It's hard to keep a good man down."

What do you get if you cross a chicken with a cow?
Roost beef.

The dentist looked into his patient's mouth, and said "The only way I can cure your bad breath is to take out all your teeth."
"Will I be able to sing in the church choir afterwards?" asked the patient.
"I don't see why not," replied the dentist.
"Well, I wasn't good enough to sing in it last time I auditioned."

What's a cow's favorite love-song?
"When I Fall In Love, It Will Be For Heifer."

"I suffered from travel sickness on the train this morning," said an absent-minded professor. "I hate traveling with my back to the engine."

"Why didn't you ask the person in the seat opposite to change with you?" asked his wife.

"I couldn't," said the professor. "The seat was empty."

At a very posh wedding, one of the guests broke wind. The bridegroom was furious and rounded on the guilty party.

"How dare you break wind in front of my wife?" he roared.

"Sorry," said the guest. "Was it her turn?"

A man walked into a chemist shop and asked for a spray that filled a room with the smell of rotten eggs, stale socks and sour milk. "What on earth do you want something like that for?" asked the chemist.

"I've got to leave my flat this morning, and it states in the lease that I must leave it exactly as I found it!"

"I see the baby's nose is running again," said a worried father.

"For goodness sake!" snapped his wife. "Can't you think of anything apart from racing?"

"Gosh, it's raining cats and dogs," said Suzie looking out of the kitchen window.

"I know," said her mother who had just come in. "I've just stepped in a poodle!"

"Keep that dog out of my garden. It smells disgusting!" a neighbor said to a small boy one day. The boy went home to tell everyone to stay away from the neighbor's garden because of the smell!

"Have you heard about the new after-shave that drives women crazy?"

"No! Tell me about it."

"It smells of 50 dollar notes."

"My husband really embarrassed me yesterday. We were at the vicarage for tea and he drank his with his little finger sticking out."

"But that's considered polite in some circles."

"Not with the teabag hanging from it, it's not."

Why couldn't the butterfly go to the dance?
Because it was a moth-ball.

A little man walked into a police station one day and said,
"I've got three big brothers and we all live in the same room. My eldest brother has seven cats. Another one has three dogs, and the third has a goat. I want you to do something about the smell."
"Are there windows in your room?" asked the duty-officer.
"Yes, of course there are!" said the man.
"Have you tried opening them?"
"What, and lose all my pigeons?"

What do you get if you cross an eagle with a skunk?
A bird that stinks to high heaven.

"What has a bottom at the top?"
"I don't know. What has a bottom at the top?"
"Your legs."

What do you get if you cross a flea with a rabbit?
Bugs Bunny.

What do we get from naughty cows?
Bad milk!

What do you get if you cross a crocodile with a flower?
I don't know, but I'm not going to smell it.

What do you get if you cross a Scottish legend and a
bad egg?
The Loch Ness pongster.

Knock, knock.
Who's there?
Dishes.
Dishes who?
Dishes the way I talk now I've got false teeth.

What smells of fish and goes round and round at 100
miles an hour?
A goldfish in a blender.

"Do you know," said the teacher to one of her pupils who had BO, "that we call you the wonder child in the staffroom?"
"Why's that, Miss?"
"Because we all wonder when you're going to wash!"

What cheese is made backward?
Edam.

"Doctor, doctor, my husband smells like a fish."
"Poor sole!"

Did you hear about the man who took his pet skunk to the cinema? During a break in the film, the woman sitting in front, who had been most affected by the animal's smell, turned round and said in a very sarcastic voice,
"I'm surprised that an animal like that should appreciate a film like this."
"So am I," said the man. "He hated the book."

What do you call a multi-story pig-pen?
A styscraper.

"Did you hear about the mad scientist who invented a gas so strong it burns its way through anything?"
"No, what about him?"
"Now he's trying to invent something to keep it in!"

"Eureka!" shouted the famous scientist when he made an important discovery.
"Sorry, professor," said his assistant. "I didn't have time to shower this morning."

Why did the pig run away from the pig-sty? He felt that the other pigs were taking him for grunted.

Did you hear about the ghoul's favorite hotel? It had running rot and mould in every room.

There was a young man called Art,
Who thought he'd be terribly smart,
He ate ten cans of beans,
And busted his jeans,
With a loud and earth-shattering ****!

"Doctor, doctor, these pills you gave me for BO ..."
"What's wrong with them?"
"They keep slipping from under my arms!"

"Can I have another slice of lemon?" a man in a pub
asked the barmaid.
"We don't have any lemons in this pub!"
"Oh no!" said the man. "If that's true, I've just
squeezed your canary into my gin and tonic!"

The eighth Earl of Jerry was showing Americans round
his ancestral home, Jerry Hall, when one of them
pointed to a moth-eaten, stuffed polar bear.
"Gee! That beast sure smells," said the American.
"Why d'ya keep it?"
"For sentimental reasons. It was shot by my mother
when she and my father were on a trip to the Arctic."
"What's it stuffed with?" asked the American.
"The seventh Earl of Jerry!"

"Your son is horribly spoiled," a woman said to a proud
mother one day.
"How dare you!" retorted the second woman. "My
son's a perfect little gentleman."
"I'm afraid you haven't seen what the steamroller's
done to him!"

"Doctor, doctor, I've had tummy ache since I ate three
crabs yesterday."
"Did they smell bad when you took them out of their
shells?"
"What do you mean 'took them out of their shells'?"

375

How can you tell if an elephant has been sleeping in your bed?
The sheets are wrinkled and the bed smells of peanuts.

What's yellow and sniffs?
A banana with a bad cold.

"Why are you crying, little boy?"
"'Cos we've just had to have our dog put down!" sobbed the lad.
"Was he mad?" asked the old lady.
"Well he wasn't too happy about it."

Did you hear about the baby skunk who asked his mother if he could have a chemistry set for Christmas?
She wouldn't let him have one in case he stank the house out.

"I say! I say! I say!
Did you hear about the taxi-driver who found a pair of kippers in the back of his cab?"
"No! Tell me about it!"
"The police told me that if no one claimed them within six months, he could have them back."

What's purple and hums?
A rotten plum!

"Daddy! Daddy! Mommy said our next-door neighbors,
the Joneses, have mice in their house."
"What on earth gave her that idea?"
"Well. You know Mr Jones is away?"
"Yes."
"When we were driving home after school, this
afternoon, Mommy saw the milkman leaving and she
said she thought she smelt a rat."

Did you hear about the boy who sat under a cow? He
got a pat on the head.

"Here's your Christmas present. A box of your favorite
chocs."
"Coo, thanks! But they're half empty!"
"Well, they're my favorite chocs too!"

Only a week after Christmas an irate Mom stormed
into the toy shop.
"I'm bringing back this unbreakable toy fire-engine,"
she said to the man behind the counter. "It's useless!"
"Surely your son hasn't broken it already?" he asked.
"No, he's broken all his other toys with it!"

"Doctor, how can I cure myself of sleepwalking?"
"Sprinkle tin-tacks on your bedroom floor."

"Are you writing a thank-you letter to Grandpa like I
told you to?"
"Yes Mom."
"Your handwriting seems very large."
"Well, Grandpa's very deaf, so I'm writing very loud."

Why are ghosts cowards?
'Cos they've got no guts.

A distraught mom rushed into the back yard, where
eight-year old Tommy was banging on the bottom of
an old upturned tin bath with a poker.
"What do you think you're playing at?" she demanded.
"I'm just entertaining the baby," explained Tommy.
"Where is the baby?" asked his Mom.
"Under the bath."

What does the Indian ghost sleep in?
A creepy teepee.

Who brings the monsters their babies?
Frankenstork.

"You're late for work again, Lamport!"
"Yes, I'm sorry sir. I overslept."
"I thought I told you to get an alarm-clock."
"I did sir, but there are nine of us in our family."
"What's that got to do with it?"
"The alarm was only set for eight!"

Young Chris was definitely more than a bit thick; when his pal asked him how he had enjoyed his day at the zoo, he replied, "It was a rotten swizz! I saw a sign that said 'To The Monkeys,' so I followed it and saw the monkeys. Then I saw another sign that said 'To The Bears,' so I followed that and saw the bears. But when I followed a sign that said 'To the Exit,' I found myself out on the street."

The box-office clerk at the theater went to the manager's office to tell him that there were two horses in the foyer. "Two horses?" exclaimed the manager in surprise. "What on earth do they want?"
"Two stalls for Monday night."

What do you think of Dracula films?
Fangtastic!

"Doctor, doctor! I'm becoming invisible!"
"Yes, I can see you're not all there."

"Doctor, doctor! You've taken out my tonsils, my adenoids, my gall-bladder, my varicose veins and my appendix, but I still don't feel well."
"That's quite enough out of you."

"Doctor, doctor! I feel like a sheep!"
"That's baaaaaad!"

"Doctor, doctor! I feel like an apple!"
"We must get to the core of this."

"Doctor, doctor! I feel like a dog!"
"Sit!"

"Doctor, doctor! I've just swallowed a pencil!"
"Sit down and write your name."

A Scotsman paying his first visit to the zoo stopped by one of the cages.
"An' whut animal would that be?" he asked the keeper. "That's a moose from Canada," came the reply. "A moose!" exclaimed the Scotsman, "Hoots – they must ha' rats like elephants over there!"

In which Biblical story is tennis mentioned?
When Moses served in Pharoah's court...

"I say waiter, there's a fly in my soup!"
"Well, throw him a doughnut – they make super lifebelts!"

381

Why do elephants have flat feet?
From jumping out of tall trees.

Is the squirt from an elephant's trunk very powerful?
Of course – a jumbo jet can keep 500 people in the air
for hours at a time.

How do you make an elephant sandwich?
First of all you get a very large loaf...

What did the fireman's wife get for Christmas?
A ladder in her stocking.

Why did the cowboy die with his boots on?
'Cos he didn't want to stub his toes when he kicked the
bucket.

"Doctor, doctor! I think I need glasses!"
"You certainly do, madam. This is a fish and chip shop.

Fantasy Stories   *Mike Ashley*   £4.99
Some of the best fantasy stories of the century. Many have been written especially for this book, others are classics.

Space Stories   *Mike Ashley*   £4.99
Around thirty exciting stories, some set on a future Earth, others on worlds far away.

True Mystery Stories   *Finn Bevan*   £4.99
Collection of thirty tales based on the world's most fascinating unexplained phenomena.

True Sea Stories   *Paul Aston*   £4.99
Tales of mystery, crime and piracy, sunken treasure, races won and lost, and silent, deadly beasts beneath the waves.

True Horror Stories   *Terrance Dicks*   £4.99
More than thirty accounts of truly terrifying experiences, including the horror of a plane crash and of being trapped underground.

True Survival Stories   *Anthony Masters*   £4.99
Gripping tales of survival against all the odds, including Apollo 13, the Andes plane crash, and many more.

Robinson books are available from all good bookshops or can be ordered direct from the publisher. Just tick the title you want and fill in the form below.

Robinson Publishing Ltd, PO Box 11, Falmouth, Cornwall TR10 9EN
Tel: +44(0) 1326 317200 Fax: +44(0) 1326 317444 Email: books@Barni.avel.co.uk

UK/BFPO customers please allow £1.00 for p&p for the first book, plus 50p for the second, plus 30p for each additional book up to a maximum charge of £3.

Overseas customers (inc Ireland) please allow £2.00 for the first book, plus £1.00 for the second, plus 50p for each additional book.

Please send me the titles ticked above.

NAME (Block letters) ....

ADDRESS ....

.... POSTCODE ....

I enclose a cheque/PO (payable to Robinson Publishing Ltd) for ....
I wish to pay by Switch/Credit Card

.... Card Expiry Date ....